# GROUP DISCUSSION

# GROUP DISCUSSION

Sannita Chakraborty Saha

PUSTAK MAHAL®

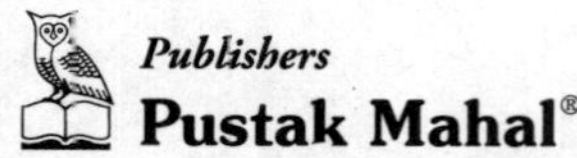

***Administrative office and sale centre***

J-3/16 , Daryaganj, New Delhi-110002
☎ 23276539, 23272783, 23272784 • *Fax:* 011-23260518
*E-mail:* info@pustakmahal.com • *Website:* www.pustakmahal.com

***Branches***

**Bengaluru:** ☎ 080-22234025 • *Telefax:* 080-22240209
*E-mail*: pustakmahalblr@gmail.com
**Mumbai:** ☎ 022-22010941, 022-22053387
*E-mail*: unicornbooksmumbai@gmail.com
**Patna:** ☎ 0612-3294193 • *Telefax:* 0612-2302719
*E-mail*: rapidexptn@gmail.com



ISBN 978-81-223-1323-9

**Edition: 2017**



***Printed at :*** AR Emm International, Delhi

This book is dedicated to my son Aarav. You are the best thing that ever happened to me......

# Acknowledgements

I thank Mr Ram Avtar Gupta, Chairman, **Pustak Mahal** for giving me the opportunity to write this book. And, a special thank you to Mr SK Roy for his constant cooperation. This would not have been possible without these two key people.

# Preface

Group Discussion is an activity wherein a group of individuals are made to sit in a group. They are given a topic or different topics to speak on. The individuals are evaluated on the logical flow and the way they bring their speech to a rationale end. It is very crucial for the reader to understand that GD is not a debate; it is more of a discussion where each participant has to speak logically on a topic.

Group Discussions today has became an essential part of the shortisting process for admission into a B-school or in a job interview. Many assume that GD is a cake walk, but believe me it is not. In any organization a manager is required to work in a group or manage a team of his own. Many a times, a Group Discussion is used as a parameter by job interviewers to assess a candidate's team management or group handling skills.

In a GD, there are four major things that need to be remembered. They are:

1. Grasp over Content
2. Communication Skills
3. Leadership Skills
4. Group Dynamics.

It is not just important to burn ones midnight oil to secure good grades in written exams, it is equally critical to prepare and succeed in a GD. There have been instances where students with extremely good scores couldn't get through good MBA colleges simply because they could not clear the GD round. It is therefore important to understand what is a GD, why GD is an important step to get into your dream B-school or dream job, and which personality traits are assessed in a GD.

*Group Discussion* is a book for students and professionals who are looking to succeed in life. This book will give you detailed information on various burning topics that are a rage today. It will help students and professions to communicate effectively on different topics. It will equip you to face interviews in qualifying examinations or job interviews.

I have compiled this book after a lot of research and discussion with several experts. Some parts of the content have been sourced from Internet websites. This book aims to help students and professionals get information on a variety of topics. These topics are most talked about on the Internet and are also frequently chosen by top-notch B-schools and HRs of various organizations in their GD sessions.

Many of our young readers may also wonder that content of this kind is there on the Internet, why read a book. Well my dear readers, this book will give the opportunity to read about 57 burning topics without taking the trouble of copy pasting the content or surfing mindlessly. There are also sample actual GD sessions which will give you a glimpse on how to present yourself. Reading this book will help you gain knowledge and since it is handy, you can carry it with you while travelling, relaxing, taking a break or simply choosing to read something sensible.

I look forward to an active interaction with all my readers. Happy reading!

# Contents


- Group Discussion – Definition 13
- Succeeding in a Group Discussion 14
- Guidelines 15
- Frequent Challenges during a GD 16
- Developing Apt Communication Skills and Body Language before facing a Group Discussion 17
- Preparing for Group Discussion 19
- Choosing Apt Topics for Group Discussion 20
- Group Discussion – Its relevance 22
- Types of Group Discussions 22
- Five Most Asked Interview Questions with Sample Answers 23

SECTION 1

01. How to deal with rising oil prices? 28
02. Is the consumer really the king in India? 32
03. Is globalization really necessary? 35
04. Indian villages – our strength or weakness? 38
05. Indian economy: old wine in new bottle 42
06. Do think the Satyam scandal would impact foreign investments in India? 45
07. Every cloud has a silver lining 49
08. Advertising is a waste of resources 51
09. Commercialization of health care: good or bad? 54
10. Are Indians less quality conscious? 57
11. Advertising is all glitter and little truth 60
12. Film-makers are indulging in cinematic exploitation in the name of folk culture 62
13. Corruption is the main outcome of democracy in India 65
14. Skilled manpower shortage in India 67
15. In our economic matters, there is an excessive tendency towards the thinking rather than doing 70
16. Are MNC's superior to Indian companies 73
17. Is it fair for banks to use force to recover loans? 76

18. Should India break diplomatic ties with Pakistan? **79**
19. Should important services like transport be left to market forces? **82**
20. Developing countries need trade, not aid **85**

## SECTION 2

01. Marriage and beyond **90**
02. Communicate to stay happily married **92**
03. Infertility **94**
04. Internet – need or curse **96**
05. Is Philosophy just an arm chair theory? **98**
06. Success is all about human relations **100**
07. Censorship is the need of the hour **102**
08. Education and success – Is there a correlation? **104**
09. We don't learn from history, we repeat it **106**
10. If there were no armies in the world...... **108**
11. Wisdom does not come with age **110**
12. Management education – Is it necessary to succeed n business **112**
13. The changing role of women in India **114**
14. NGOs – role in bringing development **116**
15. IPL **118**
16. Semesters system – boon or curse? **121**
17. Superstitions **123**
18. Bigamy **125**
19. Kids today are not what they used to be **127**
20. Examinations – has it killed education? **129**
21. Are beauty pageants necessary? **131**
22. Terrorism **133**
23. Impact of television reality shows on children **135**
24. Sex education **137**
25. Inflation **139**
26. Surrogacy **141**
27. AIDS **143**
28. Facebook **146**
29. Twitter **148**

30. Anna and Jan Lokpal Bill **150**
31. FDI in Retail in India 2011 **153**
32. Workplace problems that women employees face **155**
33. Wrongful Termination Lawyers: Angels in Shinning Armours **158**
34. Bankruptcy – A Lifeline for Debtors **160**
35. SEO....The New Tool to Enhance Your Website **162**
36. Depression: a common Ailment among youth **164**
37. Indian Hockey – Near Extinction **167**

●●

# Group Discussion – Definition

Humans are the only species created by God blessed with the ability to communicate. In communication, speech plays a crucial part. Whenever humans are in a group, there is always a need to communicate and this is when speech is the main instrument. In a Group Discussion, if you want your thoughts and ideas to make a powerful impact on the audience or on your counterparts, your speech should be razor sharp, blended with clarity, tone and diction.

A Group Discussion is a serious form of discussion wherein a group of people gets together to discuss a topic. It is a methodology, which is used by selectors to assess a prospective candidate and determine his/her ability to fit into a desired job.

These days selectors of various B-schools such as IIMs, XLRI, and Engineering Colleges such as IITs and other professional courses such as UPSC, Civil Services, Private and Public sector undertakings consider GD to be an important selection criterion. Through GD, selectors try to assess the candidates' ability to deal with strategic situations and judge their confidence level and decision-making skills.

GD is not like a formal debate. Here a group of candidates is given a topic or a situation, a few minutes to think about the same, and then asked to discuss it among themselves for about 15-20 minutes.

Professional institutes have observed over the years that students who perform well in GD's are typically those who have a consistently good academic record during their secondary school, higher secondary school, and graduate levels, besides exhibiting sufficiently high aptitude as measured by the CAT or other professional test scores. Apart from the written examination, GD/Interview performance holds about 10-20% weightage in the selection criteria. It goes without saying that these percentages are only indicative and can vary widely from institute to institute. Even for a given institute, the weightage may vary from year to year.

# Succeeding in a Group Discussion (GD)

In this competitive world, where every student and professional is looking for that extra edge, Group Discussion has become a crucial part of the filtering or selection process in admissions, recruitment, etc. Educational and professional institutes have adopted Group Discussion as a medium to elimination or for selection.

In fact it has been observed that GD has also helped in identifying top talents across the world. Group Discussions are at times led by an individual from within the institution, conducting the session, or many a times it is handled by the participants. When an individual from within the institute is conducting a GD, utmost care should be taken of one's conduct because one is judged on every parameter.

It has been observed that if participants are left alone during the GD, it gives them the liberty to express themselves to the best of their ability. It is important that you exude confidence in every situation. There may be times when the topic may not be of your comfort level or your knowledge of that topic may be limited, do not look nervous, take a deep breath, quickly think of some points that you can elaborate. At all times be confident.

# Guidelines

As a participant it is crucial that you understand that GD is a process where every participant shares his/her ideas and opinions with others in the group.

Prior to a GD, it is assumed that you realize what is expected out of you, what to speak and when to speak. Once you get the opportunity, speak or discuss accordingly and precisely.

A GD is completely a different ball game. Do not compare it to an examination, a debate competition or even a seminar. When the opportunity to speak comes, it is up to you to smartly utilize your chances and list your ideas/thoughts/opinions in an attractive manner that gets others' attention.

A GD may differ depending on the requirements. The pattern in which GD's are conducted may differ. Keep a calm mind and take it as a challenge.

There will be times when you as a participant may be asked to initiate a GD. In such a situation, you must be well-prepared to initiate the discussion. In such circumstances, you have no choice but to listen to other's presentations and then respond. Therefore, you should be careful while initiating a GD especially because you are expected to excel.

As a confident participant, do not hesitate to present your thoughts and ideas on the topic of the GD. Do it in such a manner that it appears to be clear, logical and well pronounced. You should be very clear in your mind about the topic, including the way you will present before the audience/group. In addition it is of utmost importance that you look confident of yourself and your presentation.

In a GD, avoid talking about any controversial topic that may be a personal attack on an individual, character assassination of an individual or anything that may be anti-national in nature. Avoid taking an extreme stand on anything in the GD, unless it is a compulsion.

An important rule that is applicable for all types of GD's is that your presentations should be specific to the topic. Do not deviate and drift away from the concerned topic.

Another smart move to succeed in GD's is to carefully listen to what other participants in the group are saying on the topic. This observation will help you to plan and present counter arguments and at the same time assert your position in the GD.

To succeed in a GD, it is important that you keep yourself updated with current affairs so that whatever the topic may be, you are able to speak on it and also counter the arguments.

Developing your communication skills is perhaps an extremely important step in your path to success, because presenting your thoughts and ideas for others to understand in a concise and precise manner is what is required from you.

For a participant to come out a winner in a GD it is advisable to practice mock GD sessions on few topics pertaining to current affairs, with friends or relatives. This is an all time effective formula to correct your shortcomings and also to keep yourself up to date with information.

# Frequent Challenges in a Group Discussion

It will be foolish of us to think that the path will be without any thorns. The road to success is not a very comfortable drive. If you are chosen to lead a group in a GD session, there will be a number of challenges you will have to overcome. The strategy for you and your group will be to successfully conquer these challenges. This conquest will pave the way for success or failure of your group. You have to be ready with strategies that will help you overcome these challenges.

These are some frequent challenges that are met by students and professionals. These pointers will help you prepare yourself against similar situations.

In a GD, there will be a set of 5-7 or more participants and each of them will come with their individual thoughts and ideas. As mature individuals we must ensure that no one ridicules anybody's thoughts and ideas, especially, when one is presenting to the group. It is advised to kindly avoid any kind of mockery or personal attack. When such situations occur, it slows down the productivity of the group. It makes the rest of the members cautious and conscious. They lose confidence and hesitate to speak their minds. They refuse to voice their own ideas or opinions. One great way to deal with this kind of situation is to clearly state at the onset of the session that no mockery or personal attack will be appreciated or allowed. Inform the participants at the onset that if anyone has a problem or does not agree with an idea that has been presented, he/she can come up with something better. This will help in avoiding any kind of humiliation or disagreements. As a leader, make it clear to all the members of the group that you respect and appreciate their efforts. This will give them confidence and push them to give their best.

The next challenge that you will want to overcome is ensuring that the idea or thought being discussed in the topic is not lost. As a leader, ensure that the connection is always there. Many a times when a discussion happens, members tend to drift from the main idea or thought to different tangents. To avoid this disconnect, it is important for the participants to maintain that connection regarding the idea/thought that is being discussed. A common hitch that is seen in GDs is that participants tend to build newer ideas rather than adding to the existing idea that is being discussed by another participant. Often, these ideas or thoughts will show no relation to the newer ideas presented. When such a situation arises, then the whole discussion goes awry. The central idea or thought fails to develop because of the overlap of the new ideas.

In such circumstances, it is the leader of the group who has to pull the strings. It is he who will have to bring the car back on to the track. In an ideal situation, a few participants come up with great ideas, and others simply contribute to it rather than pulling the chord in a different direction. If such a situation arrives, when your Group Discussion is not going the way it should, you as a leader should ask any one member to share an idea or solution that can help to resolve the issue. Once the idea or solution is presented, you can ask the remaining participants to comment on that without generating any new ideas.

The next challenge before you is to keep your ears open for any information. This is often found to be challenging, as you as a participant have to be alert so as not to lose the connection between ideas. It is crucial that when you are presenting your idea/opinion, you are able to summarize what you have heard. When all participants are able to do this, it will help the group to come to a conclusion or find a way. Summarizing information may not seem an easy task for all participants as it is a skill one must possess. What is needed of all the participants is to go over the core idea of the discussion and summarize any points that have been brought up.

Keeping one's ears open for important ideas is not just the leader's role but of all the members of the group. If everyone in the group is found to be attentive, the response to ideas will be faster.

If the participants are not listening to the ideas being presented, there will be no effective response from them. This will be a hurdle regarding the participants' ability to come up with ideas

Once these challenges are overcome, the Group Discussion will be effective.

# Developing Apt Communication Skills and Body Language before facing a Group Discussion

When it comes to the total scores, it is the right etiquette and body language among other things, that helps you reaching the next level. Much of this has nothing to do with your subject matter, expertise or experience. So, in this chapter, we shall cover some aspects of etiquette, with special emphasis on body language and communication skills.

# During the GD

## Greeting the board

In the West, people usually greet each other with a handshake, even in formal settings. But in India, this may not always be a good idea. Whereas a formal "Good morning," "Good afternoon" or a namaskar maybe considered proper, a bow, a nod and a greeting is a safe strategy under most circumstances. If, however, the speaker extends his or her hand, you must shake hands.

## Sitting

In a Group Discussion, one feels tense, nervous and vulnerable at the same time. A table acts as a barrier and sometimes reassures you. In general you should play safe – don't sit unless asked to. If someone keeps you waiting or forgets to offer a seat, you may politely ask "May I take a seat?" Smile and establish eye contact with all the speakers.

Body language plays a vital role in interviews and Group Discussions. Recruiters don't select on the basis of resume alone. Researchers have found that interviewers mostly make up their minds in the first few minutes and body language plays a very important role in this first impression.

## Voice and Delivery

Knowing is not enough. Communicating your ideas and skillset in a proper fashion can work wonders for you.

Many of us find it difficult to convey our ideas, especially if we have trouble speaking English. Unfortunately there is no easy solution to it. You have to learn the language and build your confidence gradually. Try to speak even if you make mistakes. Unless you do so, you will not be able to get your ideas across.

A few tips like the use of simple words and short sentences might help you, especially if you are not very confident about speaking in English.

You need not worry much about your voice. It is something natural. But continuous practice in front of the mirror or the use of voice recorder might be beneficial.

You might have a very good command over the English language. You may be a flawless speaker. You may even have a good voice. But how you deliver is what finally matters.

Be careful of your punctuation marks even while you speak. Try avoiding the pauses like 'hmm...' or 'eh...' during a GD. It might cast a negative impression on the panel.

# Preparing for Group Discussion

The first and foremost task before you, before a Group Discussion, is to prepare yourself. Read on a variety of topics like current affairs, international news, sports, cinema, etc. Educational and professional institutes, HR firms, BPOs, management institutes come up with innovative topics to judge the participants' caliber. So it is important to read on a variety of things.

Secondly, it is important to be prepared because, being prepared will allow you to communicate effectively. This will give you confidence and an upper hand over the other participants. Also it will give the participants an ability to learn concepts or solve problems.

A Group Discussion cannot succeed without the participants using any reasoning. It is important that participants ask questions. The ability to reason will help you understand how much the other participants know about a specific topic. This ability will help you to analyze their knowledge. Asking specific questions will help you to learn more about the other participants as well.

If you are the leader of a GD, it is your responsibility to ensure that there are no conflicts. Conflicts kill the essence of a GD. It makes the entire purpose of the discussion unproductive. Avoid making statements that gives your personal opinion on any comment or idea of another participant. Avoid statements like "I think that is an excellent idea." This is because such comments from your end may send a message implying that all other ideas are irrelevant.

Avoid being over generous and overtly helpful. If participants are asked to collect information, stop yourself from going all the way to provide them that information. Your initiative will hamper their ability to conduct their own research. If you are the leader, it is your responsibility to ensure that every participant contributes to the discussion.

A GD is a group activity, so it is important that all members of the group participate in the discussion. As a leader, if you observe that one of the participants is not participating in the discussion, go an extra mile and ask him/her what he/she thinks about the idea or thought. It is important for everyone to feel like they belong to the group.

It is important to make sure everyone is discussing the topic. The students should talk and make statements regarding the topic. Everyone should be able to voice their own opinion. The best way to approach the topic of discussion is to start with a concept that is simple, before moving to one that is complex. While you don't want the member to become bored, you also don't want the topic to become so complicated that no one gains anything from it. Whenever people get together in a group, there will be interpersonal issues among some of the members. Each person will have a different personality type, and some will not work well with others.

If you see a potential problem, deal with it before it becomes a major issue that disrupts the Group Discussion. Whenever you observe that any participant is drifting away from the central idea or thought, it is important that you bring that participant back to the core topic. Any kind of diversion on part of the participants should be avoided. For a successful GD, if you notice that a few participants are facing problems with reasoning, or expressing their ideas or thoughts, you must help them.

To be well-prepared for a Group Discussion, ensure you are prepared on a variety of topics. Once the topic is announced understand the topic of the discussion, and if necessary, do a quick research on it, if the situation allows it. Once you have done the necessary research on the topic, you should develop your own thoughts and opinions.

When all the people in a group are prepared, it allows the discussion to go to the right direction. However, when they are not prepared, it becomes very difficult to achieve the goals. To be successful in a Group Discussion, you must know how to work well with others, and understand the topic to be discussed.

# Choosing Apt Topics for Group Discussion

A Group Discussion is often defined as a process wherein a group of people get together to exchange experiences, information, ideas, or their thoughts. In a GD, the participants are working towards a common goal. Group Discussions are also considered to be an excellent way to help participants learn to express their ideas and thoughts.

However, most Group Discussions have a tendency to be formal rather than mere conversations. The topics discussed in this book pertain to Group Discussions conducted in various educational and professional institutes, HR departments, etc., holding GD as selection criteria. It is important to select the right topic, which every participant can relate to and also would be interested in. When a selected topic for discussion is thrown at the group, it is crucial that the topic is clear to all participating.

Appropriate topics will allow participants to come up with their own questions or statements. Whenever a topic is presented to the group, it should be in the form of a question. In most cases, open-ended questions prove to be fruitful.

For example:

Is coalition politics here to stay?

Does India need a dictator?

Is India moving away from a secularist state?

What ails Indian sports?

Is Philosophy just an armchair theory?

Is success is all about human relations?

Borderless worlds – A dream or reality?

Is quality a myth in India?

Education and success – Is there a correlation?

We don't learn from history, we repeat it...why?

When it comes to choosing the topic for GD, the topic should be relevant on different levels, and should be able to engage all the participants. It is important that all the participants are able to build on the topic. When the topic is presented, all participants should be given time to think and prepare it. This allows them to come up with ideas or solutions that can be helpful. During a GD, the topic should be something that will allow participants to fall back on past knowledge.

But what is critical is the fact that the topic chosen should allow the participants to think. When interesting topics are presented before the participants, they are able to collect their thoughts on the topic. This way they are able to come up with significant ideas. What is important to note here is that all the participants should be given the right to ask their own questions, as long as they are correlated to the topic.

The size of the group is also important. In case there are many participants, it is advisable to split the group into five people. A smaller group allows participants to interact with each other. Larger groups are difficult to manage, and the level of interaction within the group is also limited. Group activities give the opportunity to perform different tasks. Everyone should understand the tasks that they are required to perform. GDs if held on regular basis, can prove to be useful for all participants as they can take turns between roles. This will help each of them gain experience by carrying out a number of different tasks.

Once the topic is decided upon, procedures should be established for the group which can help them achieve a certain goal. It is important that all participants are made to realize that the best interests of the group should come first instead of their individual self. All participants should listen to the ideas and opinions of other members, irrespective of the fact that they may not agree with the points raised by the others.

# Group Discussion – Its Relevance

Group Discussion as a selection process is excellent as well as vital because it makes each participant independent. Apart from independence, it also teaches them to work in a group. Though individuals in the group will work together to come up with ideas or solutions, they can also act independently by supporting the group. GD allows participants to develop collaboration skills. This skill set is what is needed in a manager or a team member when he/she joins an organization. GD also allows the institute or HR to evaluate the participants, and especially the leader of the group to see if he/she is able to work with each member on an individual level.

# Types Of Group Discussions

## 1. Topic-based GDs are further classified into:-

(a) Factual topics are about practical things, which an ordinary person is aware of in his day-to-day life. Typically these are about socio-economic issues. These can be current, i.e., they may have been in the news lately, or could be unbound by time. A factual topic for discussion gives candidates the chance to prove that they are aware of and sensitive to their environment.

For example, the Education Policy of India, Tourism in India or State of the Aged in the Nation, etc.

(b) Controversial topics are the ones that are argumentative in nature. They are meant to generate controversy. In GDs where these topics are given for discussion, the noise level is usually high and there may be tempers flying. The idea behind giving a topic like this is to see how much maturity the candidates are displaying by keeping their tempers in check, by rationally and logically arguing their point of view without getting personal and emotional. Some of these topics include, Reservations should be removed, Women make better Managers, etc.

(c) Abstract topics are about intangible things. These topics are not given often for discussion, but their possibility cannot be ruled out. These topics test the candidates' lateral thinking and creativity.

For example, A is an alphabet, Twinkle Twinkle Little Star, the number 10, etc.

**2. Case-based GDs** use a case instead of a topic. The case study tries to simulate a real-life situation. Information about the situation will be given to the candidates and they would be asked as a group to resolve the situation. In the case study there are no incorrect answers or perfect solutions. The objective in the case study is to get them to think about the situation from various angles.

IIM Ahmedabad, IIM Indore and IIT SOM Mumbai have a case-based discussion rather than topic-based discussion in their selection procedures.

## 3. Open GD

An Open GD follows a loose format in which any of the participant can begin with the discussion. There is a fight for survival in an Open GD as one may not get a chace to speak at all. There are good chances of finding out the leadership potential and team-based skills in an Open GD, but it might also get tough for the evaluators to came to a possible decision in an Open GD.

## 4. Closed GD

There is always a sequence or order that is generated in a Closed GD. Discussants speak accordingly as everyone gets a break. Closed GD is more effective in observing communication, conceptualization and insight. Here there is not much scope for exploring interpersonal skills. Evaluation comes early here.

# Five Most Asked Interview Questions with Sample Answers

## Question 1: So, tell us about yourself?

Undoubtedly the most frequently asked interview question, and one that interviewees have the most difficulty answering. Your answer should be in alignment with your career objective, which means you shouldn't respond with comments about your hobbies, spouse or extra-curricular activities.

1. Start with a brief introduction. Talk about skills that are key to the position applied for. e.g. : Here the positiion applied for is Sales Executive

*Sample: During my 2 years of experience as a sales executive, I have mastered the ability to prospect, generate business leads, and motivate my team members to reach targets. I look forward to achieving this in my next job venture as well.*

2. Provide a summary of your recent work history. Keep your response limited to your current experience. Don't go back more than 2 years.

*Sample: 'Most recently, at The XYZ Corporation, I was challenged with turning around a stagnant territory that ranked last in sales. I developed an aggressive sales campaign that focused on winning new accounts and nurturing the existing client base. Within six months, my sales team and I were able to increase sales by 40 per cent.'*

3. Tie your response to the needs of the organization. Demonstrate how your experience and skills are transferable to the open position.

*Sample: 'I have learnt about the challenges your IT department is facing and my background in developing software for leading companies will add value.'*

4. Ask an engaging question. By asking a question, you gain control of the interview. Doing so will alleviate the stress you may feel to perform. But make sure your question does not bounce back on you.

*Sample: 'What strategies are currently underway to reduce the employee turnover and improve morale?'*

## Question 2: What are your greatest strengths and weaknesses?

Highlighting strengths and accomplishments: Use specific examples to highlight your accomplishments – explicit numbers, results and outcomes. Generic words are meaningless unless backed by data. For example, instead of using the word 'significant', use a number or percentage instead.

Talk about the times you may have sacrificed a vacation to complete an important project.

Quote an example from a past job where you drove the meeting, committee or project that was languishing. Or, when a deadline loomed and you came up with a way to reach the goal.

Show how curiosity has served you well in the last job. Talk about how you were able to see the broader consequences of a decision in your previous company. Your contribution provided a viewpoint that others had overlooked.

*Sample: I have determined a new perspective to my career. I am confident to my excellent negotiation skills which I have honed through the years. During years of working as sales person, I accumulated valuable experiences and gained essential skills. I have even sacrificed my vacations and have worked overtime zealously to complete my targets and deadlines.*

The one question candidates love to avoid is, “What is your greatest weakness?” Do not give superficial answers like “I’m a workaholic” or “I’m a perfectionist.” These are boring and predictable. Interviewers can even reply to them with, “That doesn’t sound like a weakness. Now why don’t you tell me about a real weakness?” So, state a true weakness that doesn’t have a major impact on your ability to do the job.

*Sample: If you are applying for a non-managerial role: ‘In the past, I’ve had some trouble sharing responsibilities with others. I felt I could do things better and faster myself. This sometimes backfired because I’d end up with more than I could handle and the quality of my work would suffer. But I plan to take courses in time management and effective delegation.’*

## Question 3: Why did you leave your last job?

If you left your last job under less-than-ideal circumstances, you probably dread this question. Here’s how to handle it. Never lie. If you were fired, don’t say you quit. A background check will reveal this lie easily. Don’t say anything negative about your former boss, co-workers or company. Any negativity, frustration or anger will only reflect negatively on you.

*Sample* – If you were fired for not adhering to a company policy: *‘I was asked to leave for violating a company policy that I feel wasn’t communicated to me clearly. I should have taken the responsibility to read all of the company policies and ask questions about those I didn’t fully understand. That will be the first thing I do in my next job.’*

Any employer would love to hear stories about how employees take responsibility for their actions and learn from their mistakes. Make sure they understand that what happened to cause you to leave your last job was the exception, not the rule. Provide references or letters of recommendation to verify that your job performance is above par.

## Question 4: Why should we hire you?

Before you attend this interview question: Assume this to be your last chance to prove your worth and then take the initiative to attend this question and tell your real answers.

*Sample: First of all, I am academically qualified for this job.*

*I am confident in what I do and how I do it; and am open to feedback about my work. I take responsibility for what I do and credit a person for what I learn from him/her.*

*I am good at working by myself, but in the recent years have adapted myself to working with a team as well. This is my biggest asset.*

*I would like to add that I am optimistic even during the most challenging situations, which helps me to work stress-free.*

## Question 5: Why is it important to define a target market for your product?

In marketing if you have no target it's not like the motivational speech of "Shoot for the moon if you miss, you'll land among the stars." It just doesn't work that way in business. You'll be shooting into the black expanses of space – where no one exists.

We should sit down and look at what we are offering and look around at who we think would be perfect for our product or service.

We need to know exactly who our customers are.

It's called demographics. It's part of the research we need to do before going into business. It may not go well if we have no idea who we are going to be talking to about your service or product.

If we try to blanket everyone with one marketing message we'll lose over half of your audience simply because it doesn't apply to them.

Target who you are after and you will know how to reach them easier and find that you won't have to invest so much into your marketing to get the results you want.

## Question 6: How would you...? (Problem solving question)

The interviewers aren't looking for a 'right' or 'wrong' answer to this one. They are more interested in understanding your thought process. Show your ability to think logically and demonstrate problem-solving capabilities by:

1. Asking questions to confirm exactly what the interviewer is looking for.
2. Explaining how you would collect the information and data required to develop a solution.
3. Telling them how you'd use the information you gathered to develop and analyse alternative courses of action.
4. Sharing your solution or recommendation, explaining how you feel it's the best option based on the information you were given.

So, go ahead and create a smashing impression. It's all about the right answers.

# SECTION 1

In this section five participants are involved in a Group Discussion, on various given topics. These are samples of actual Group Discussions. I have used them to help you get a grasp of what an actual GD is all about.

Activity: Each reader is supposed to evaluate the knowledge of the speakers, assess their confidence and presentation skills. The first one has been solved for you.

Remember! In a GD, don't wait for your turn to speak, find an opportunity to put in your point of view.

Be confident!

1. How to deal with rising oil prices?
2. Is the consumer really the king in India?
3. Is globalization really necessary?
4. Indian villages – our strength or weakness?
5. Indian economy: old wine in new bottle
6. Do think the Satyam scandal would impact
   foreign investments in India?
7. Every cloud has a silver lining
8. Advertising is a waste of resources
9. Commercialization of health care: good or bad?
10. Are Indians less quality conscious?
11. Advertising is all glitter and little truth
12. Film-makers are indulging in cinematic exploitation in the name of folk culture
13. Corruption is the main outcome of democracy in India
14. Skilled manpower shortage in India
15. In our economic matters, there is an excessive tendency towards the thinking rather than doing
16. Are MNC's superior to Indian companies
17. Is it fair for banks to use force to recover loans
18. Should India break diplomatic ties with Pakistan?
19. Should important services like transport
    be left to market forces?
20. Developing countries need trade, not aid

# How to deal with Rising Oil Prices?

## Speaker 1

Rising oil prices or fuel prices is a burning issue. There are some solutions to this problem though. Why not try to switch off your car when at a red signal? The government has made its share of contribution in the name of giving the *aam janata* ideas on how to save fuel. That would be opting for car pool, CNG, etc. But the main problem in India is the Indian mentality. People in India refuse to walk a few meters even though the distance to their destination is less! They would rather pull out their swanky cars even if it is a few kilometers drive to the park. Imagine going to the park for your morning jog in your car.

Some of the major problems that are leading to the decline of oil are:

1. Poverty
2. High population
3. Over consumption and exploitation of resources
4. Low economic growth

An easy and cost-effective way to handle rising oil prices is going GREEN today. This will help us save on money and also contribute towards a better environment, or else in the future our kids will have to ride bicycles for kilometers on end.

## Speaker 2

The only way to deal with the rising oil prices is by switching to public transportation. This is primarily for that section of people who cannot survive without their cars or motorbikes or scooters. The saddest part is that more and more people are opting for multiple cars per household. This is leading to more usage of petrol/diesel. Public transport helps by becoming a common source of transportation for many people instead of a single individual burning precious fuel. We can also deal with rising oil prices by using renewable energy sources like solar power, wind, etc.

I would like to inform my dear friends that the Indian Government has several reasons behind the price hike. It has to pay $16 billion as subsidy to meet the needs of the poor and needy. Oil companies such as IOCL are compromising on their profits to provide these products at lesser rates. We may blame these companies and the government but we also have to realize that they are also helpless as they survive on the basic phenomenon of demand and supply which decides the price index of a commodity.

So let's work towards a healthy, wealthy and prosperous Indian economy.

## Speaker 3

Friends, I understand that the issue of accelerating prices of petrol and diesel in the Indian oil market is a serious matter. The morning newspaper is often the bearer of the bad news and the first thing we do is blame the government for yet again burning a hole in the *aam aadmi's* pocket. The exponential increase in the price of crude oil in the international market is the main reason, not to forget we are ourselves responsible for this calamity as well. I am sure as educated, alert and good citizens we all know that petrol and diesel are non-renewable sources of energy. If we carelessly use these resources, we will simply ruin and deplete the future of coming generations. Cursing the government does not help to decrease the price of petrol or diesel, and let's not forget it is the government who provides subsidy on consumer goods such as petrol, diesel, LPG, kerosene, etc.

Another point, which I would like to mention and remind my dear friends, is that our country has no oil wells. We import from other countries and there is also an import cost involved, which is another reason for price rise.

Coal is available in our country itself, but coal is a non-renewable source of energy. Coal will be available to us as a natural product up to 2030, so we should reduce the usage of non-renewable sources and move on to renewable sources of energy.

## Speaker 4

We all know that fuel is a non-renewable form of energy. We have limited resources and this limited resource cannot be renewed by any means. So we should avoid using our vehicles for short distances. This will not only save fuel, it will be good for the vehicles. When we are at traffic signals we must consciously switch off the engine. This helps to save fuel. Increase in fuel prices has its direct impact on other things related with fuel. For example, when diesel prices go up, prices of vegetables, fruits also go up as the trucks that run inter-state increase their carrying charges. It is like a chain reaction. One leads to another. We must realize that as Indian citizens we must make an effort to make our personal contributions that will benefit the country as a whole.

## Speaker 5

Well friends, whatever I wanted to say about this topic has already been spoken by the other participants. I have therefore nothing new to add.

## Analysis

| | |
|---|---|
| **Speaker 1:** | Confident and composed. Talked and placed strong and logical arguments. |
| **Speaker 2:** | To the point, thought provoking and decent presentation. |
| **Speaker 3:** | Sound knowledge and good points |
| **Speaker 4:** | Repetitive information, nothing new to add. |
| **Speaker 5:** | Should have added more information, instead of simply passing off. |

## Winning Strategy

In a Group Discussion, the skills judged are:

| PERSONALITY | |
|---|---|
| KNOWLEDGE | |
| COMMUNICATION SKILL | |
| LEADERSHIP | |

# Is consumer really the King in India?

## Speaker 1

This concept was earlier deeply rooted in the western and developed economies but now India is slowing adopting it, though it is yet to take a stronghold. In the 21st century with so many MNCs and new entrepreneurs erupting and taking the Indian Economy by storm, the new businessman has started thinking that the consumer is king but what about the conventional businesses in India and the Government? Are they ready to accept the fact that yes its time for us to treat the customer as the king? The pre-91 era lacked awareness of the customer demands. This was a phase when the customer was neglected. However, the liberated India is trying its best to get a hold on the customer and customer needs. This awareness has led to the formation of consumer-based structured companies. This motto clearly indicates that the consumer is king.

If we look at the West, the best instance of consumer is king can be seen in the customer service of Starbucks and Subway. The kind of food available in these chains is customer based. So in India, though the idea of consumer is king is slowly trying to get its hold, companies if they want to hold the customer's attention have to treat the customer as the king and not forget that in the long run, this will prove to be the most important aspect for the growth of the Indian Economy.

## Speaker 2

I agree with speaker 1, when he says that India after 1991 is different from India before 1991. Before 1991, the consumer was not the king. Well-known products were recognized by their brand names such as Bajaj (often referred with scooters), Fiat and Ambassador (cars), Crown and Sharp (TVs). There are instances when there were lottery systems for buying cars and a waiting period for getting a product.

After 1991, things had changed for the better. A lot of the credit goes to the new government that opened the doors for MNCs and international brands. These companies provided consumers information on the quality/cost of the product. The consumer was provided after-sales services for the durables they purchased. The consumer soon realized that goods and services came together. These MNCs gave them a wide range of products to choose from and treated their customers the same way they would like to be treated. In brief, they treated the customer as the king.

And further, the power of the consumer began to grow. There have been instances of automobile manufacturers withdrawing certain products, in the recent past, from the market due to manufacturing defects. This is a great change from the consumer's perspective. Companies are setting up special customer service desks and offering after-sales services to retain customers. Customer loyalty and customer repurchase is on top priority for most progressive brands. The consumer may not be the king in the treatment that he receives just yet, but the time is not far when he will be the king.

## Speaker 3

The two speakers have added a new perspective to this interesting topic. But in my opinion the Indian consumer is blind. The corporate sector tends to seek undue advantage of the consumer's inability to distinguish between good and bad. Manufacturers are churning out products in large varieties and in different price ranges to suit all segments of the society. This is a strategic move on part of the corporate to cater to different customers by meeting customized demands. But at the same time the quality is adulterated. This may seem a little disappointing, but I would like to add that sadly the consumers are not smart enough to determine how they are manipulated. If you look at the morning newspaper, you will be amazed to see a large number of pages dedicated to advertisements screaming of discounts, offers, etc.

These are different marketing gimmicks that corporate adapts to draw customers. Customers continue to buy products that offer attractive packaging and goods promoted by our favourite celebrity and forget to check for the real stuff. When we buy products influenced by such things so why blame the manufactures.

## Speaker 4

I have heard similar discussions on the TV several times. How is this going to help me in my life? This discussion is not going to help me get a job.

## Speaker 5

Dear friends, I completely agree with speaker 3. I feel that though the consumer has the power of a king he/she doesn't act like one. Advertisements endorsed by their favourite celebrity often carry them away. For a certain section of customers, quality hardly matters. The psychology that is predominant in this section of consumers is that if a celebrity is endorsing a product then undoubtedly the product is the best. The manufacturer takes the benefit of the consumers' foolishness. They disguise the terms and conditions attached to an offer of a product. As a strategy they tap the pulse of the consumer and use it to their benefit. The consumer in spite of being educated and aware still falls for these antics. Before making a purchase a consumer should analyze the pros and cons of that product. This way the consumer can truly become a king. To give the consumer his kingly powers, the government has set up consumer courts for the consumer's rights. *JAGO GRAHAK JAGO*. Think before you invest. This is the new motto now.

## Analysis

| | |
|---|---|
| **Speaker 1:** | Interesting speech/draws a comparison between the Indian and the Western economy. |
| **Speaker 2:** | Charts interesting examples. |
| **Speaker 3:** | Quite assertive and manages to raise some good points. |
| **Speaker 4:** | Unprofessional approach. Should have added examples. |
| **Speaker 5:** | Very reasonable and precise. To the point. |

## Winning Strategy

If you are initiating the discussion, you could do so by collectively addressing the group as "friends". Subsequently, you could use names (if the group has had a round of self-introduction prior to starting the discussion and you remember the names) or simply use pronouns like "he" or "she".

# Is Globalization really Necessary?

## Speaker 1

I completely agree with the topic that globalization is necessary for an economy to grow. The integration of economic, technological, socio-political factors with the world is known as globalization. To understand the concept of globalization, it would be an added advantage to learn about mutual co-operation and assistance and the law of comparative advantage.

Globalization is needed to reduce poverty in a country. There are several evidences and records that support this thought. Often a question arises who needs globalization? The answer lies in the fact that developing countries need globalization to become developed countries. India's wealth is its availability of skilled manpower resources, which attracts other countries to invest in India. India may not on its own have sufficient funds/money to invest in large industrial or other infrastructural developments, so it invites other countries to invest in its projects. In order to draw developed countries to India, and convince them to invest foreign funds, it has to project advantageous situations for them such as, employment, infrastructure development, tourism, foreign exchange, etc.

Most of the countries would have been reeling in depression if not for globalization. For example, where petroleum is concerned, most countries are on the verge of depleting their entire reserves and some countries don't have it at all. Seeing this, if not for globalization the entire world would be left crippled due to the massive energy crisis facing them.

However, the evidence is very convincing that developing countries believe that globalization helps growth and reduces poverty level faster than those that do not. A recent study of developing countries reported that developing economies with globalization as their strategy have shown that real incomes and output grew faster, on an average about four times faster, than inward looking economies' output.

## Speaker 2

Well, I think globalization has become an essential part of all the developing nations; for their economy to grow and be able to compete at the international platform. Where culture is concerned, adapting or retaining is hardly related with globalization because to even retain that culture we need to be economically strong and widely accepted. While preparing a delicacy it is important to use the right ingredients in appropriate quantities. Same goes with globalization, it needs to be formed or rather put forward in such a way that it helps our nation to establish itself as a developed nation.

## Speaker 3

Globalization describes a process by which regional economies, societies, and cultures have become integrated through a global network of communication, transportation, and trade. The term is sometimes used to refer specifically to economic globalization: the integration of national economies into the international economy through trade, foreign direct investment, capital flows, migration, and the spread of technology. However, globalization is usually recognized as being driven by a combination of economic, technological, socio-cultural, political, and biological factors. The term can also refer to the transnational circulation of ideas, languages, or popular culture through acculturation.

## Speaker 4

I want to begin by saying that globalization has its pros and cons. But it cannot be denied that the impact it has had on our country has been positive. It has helped Indian companies to become more competitive and ensured survival of the fittest. Though, policies should be framed to protect the interest of consumers and there should be restraint in opening the market at least in some sectors.

## Speaker 5

I do not have much knowledge on this topic. I cannot speak much on this.

## Analysis

| | |
|---|---|
| **Speaker 1:** | Confident. Talked and placed strong, logical arguments |
| **Speaker 2:** | A decent presentation. |
| **Speaker 3:** | Quite precise and to the point. |
| **Speaker 4:** | Raises some good points but does not elaborate. |
| **Speaker 5:** | Should have added at least something instead of just backing off. |

## Winning Strategy

A Group Discussion helps to evaluate leadership skills.

The ability to take leadership roles and to lead, inspire, and carry the team along to help them achieve the group's objectives.

**Example:** To be able to initiate the Group Discussion, or to be able to guide the group especially when the discussion begins losing relevance. Try to encourage all members to participate in the discussion.

# Indian villages
# – our Strength or Weakness?

## Speaker 1

India is what it is because of its rural life. Even after India has made immense progress, real India exists in the villages. According to me, villages are the backbone of our country and without villages we are nowhere. Generations have their roots in the village and not to forget, we get our necessities such as rice, wheat, barley, corn, etc., only from the villages. Apart from the food products, villages also bring us close to nature. However, villages have their own drawbacks too. Lack of basic amenities, infrastructure, and education are major issues that are holding villages from matching up to the cities. There are no proper hospitals or schools. Illiteracy and casteism are some major problems that have infested the villages of India. It is now on the government to take adequate steps to develop villages and bring them at par with the cities. We as individuals should take it on us to work for the betterment of the villages in whatever way we can. This can be by imparting adult education, educating villagers on health and welfare, eradicating casteism and by bringing proper healthcare to the villages.

## Speaker 2

I do not regard villages as our weakness. In fact, it is the urban people who are the weakness. I agree with Speaker 1 and consider the villages of India to be the country's strength. 80% of the village population's occupation is primarily agriculture. That means apart from feeding its own countrymen, a large amount of agricultural products are exported to various countries that bring in foreign revenue. India's main occupation over the years has always been agriculture and it has been a matter of pride for the nation.

For common people like you and me, villages are India's strength but for corporate and MNCs, they are a weakness. Most MNCs and real-estate companies opt for large-scale land acquisition for various projects. So they look towards the villages where vast stretches of land are available and that too at not very steep prices. They try to convince the villagers to part with their lands with hopes for better employment and growth. This leads to the destruction of the rural beauty and fresh air. With these options coming to the villages comes pollution, and if this continues then someday the big industries will occupy all the green fields and our villages will became concrete jungles. Villages are our strength and we should let it be the way it is.

An example of this is what happened in Singur in West Bengal when the Tatas wanted to start their new factory. It did bring hope of employment and may be a better state of affairs for the poor but what of the land and the livelihood of thousands of villagers?

Look at what has happened to Greater Noida, Noida, Gurgaon, Bhiwadi, etc. These areas have now become commercialized. The beautiful, lush green fields have given way to concrete buildings. With over population, there is lack of enough housing facilities so the real estate agents are moving towards villages and bringing the crowds there.

## Speaker 3

I think villages have their own strengths. When we talk of strength, the first thing that comes to each of our minds is the agricultural aspect. As my friends have already stated, about 80% of people in villagers are farmers and their main occupation is agriculture. All our grains come from the villages and so do our fruits and vegetables. Another aspect that draws many people towards the villages is the clear climate. Absence of pollution has helped villages retain their freshness and rustic feel. As for the government, because of the availability of land it has decided to build SEZ (Special Economic Zone) for industries to generate employment.

This proves that Indian villages act as the backbone of India and there should be ample support from the government for their growth in terms of roads, transportation, infrastructure, clean water, education, etc.

## Speaker 4

Indian villages lack in development which has proved a major problem for India over the years. Absence of privatized banks in villages had handicapped the villagers over the years. Because of the excess power that the rich landlords have over the poor and impoverished villagers, they have always been economically backward. This economic backwardness reflected on India's position in front of the world. Another weakness is lack of educational facilities in the villages. India has been fighting for literacy all these years but the rural mentality has been holding it back. There are villages in India where the literacy rate is as low as 10%. How can India grow if there is no education? Lack of education and financial security causes lack of confidence in people of Indian villages. So it is for the government to come up with schemes for higher education and programs of economic relief in forms of bank loans, etc.

## Speaker 5

Villages are and were always India's weakness. I think villages portray the poorer side of India, whereas India is a rich country. We are the third largest economy in the world. But because of casteism, neglect on part of the government and lack of education, the improved economy has not done any good to the development of the villages. And because of this when India is represented as a nation, Indian villages and their poor development is always debated on.

| | Analysis |
|---|---|
| **Speaker 1:** | Points out the positive and negative aspects of Indian villages. |
| **Speaker 2:** | Quite confident and bold. Raises some good points. |
| **Speaker 3:** | Sound knowledge and good points. |
| **Speaker 4:** | Placed strong logical arguments. |
| **Speaker 5:** | Though a short one, but clever. |

## Winning Strategy

### Communication Skills

The participating candidates will be assessed in terms of clarity of thought, expression, and aptness of language. One key aspect is listening. It indicates a willingness to accommodate others views.

**Example:** To be able to use simple language and explain concepts clearly so that it is easily understood by all. You actually get negative marks for using esoteric jargons in an attempt to show off your knowledge.

# Indian Economy: Old Wine in a New Bottle

## Speaker 1

I completely agree that Indian economy is old wine in new bottle. The politicians of pre and post independence continue to have similar thinking processes. They still continue to target on getting sympathy from the people. The way of execution to achieve their goals has changed though.

The government seems to be groping in the dark. It has unclear vision and when challenges are presented before them, it emerge to be directionless and has no idea how to tackle the challenges that confront the country.

The two important sectors of the Indian economy are agriculture and small-scale industries. In recent years these sectors have been treated shabbily by policies that are heavily loaded against them. The new agricultural policy announced in the past year instead of helping the agricultural sector, only aggravated the crisis. India's agriculture is now at a crossroads. Inadequate production of food grains and failure to keep pace with the high growth in population is perhaps the most depressing economic trend in India today.

Finally I would like to conclude by saying that although the common objective or goal still continues to exist, yet the way of executing those goals have changed over the past years.

## Speaker 2

This is an extremely challenging topic for me. Currently India is considered to be the third leading economy in the world, as mentioned by my dear friend, yet it has the ability to become the largest economy in the coming years. The country has grown three-fold because of its economic policies in the recent years. However, if we compare India with China, both countries got their independence around the same time, yet China is always two steps ahead in every field.

The prime reason is corruption, which is digging a hole in the country's heart. It is not that other countries are devoid of corruption but the ratio varies. The amount of scams that are reported every other day is not only killing the country's reputation but is also affecting the country's economic growth. Think about the amount of black money that is deposited in the Swiss bank accounts of our politicians, if this amount is invested in the development of our country, it could do much for us.

When the ruling party changes its policies and looks beyond filling its own pockets, then only will the new wine will be found in a new bottle of our economy.

## Speaker 3

India is full of corrupt politicians and till the time they are ruling the country, our economy will not match up to that of the US or any other country. If we want the Indian economy to prosper and match up to that of other countries, we need youngsters like us who will think of the nation and not of themselves.

## Speaker 4

Wine tastes better as it grows older just as old minds come up with good ideas if they work correctly. Old brains have experience in facing several problems and from them they learned things, which came in handy when bigger things are planned. But in India, corruption plays a very crucial role in every political sphere. Even if a political leader wants to achieve the desirable economy rate, others may not agree. For example: Dr Manmohan Singh's decision to withdraw the nuke deal with the US, which met with opposition from the other leaders.

## Speaker 5

Dear friends I agree with all of you. Indian economy is not in the hands of the politicians and we should not put all the blame on them because we the citizens of India democratically elect our government. So it is on us to vote for the right people and bring an honest government to power. In India, ironically, if an honest and people-dedicated government wants to bring a change, the opposition ensures that the new government goes out of power or that the change only brings negative results. Similarly, if a government employee wants to do something different or positive, he is transferred to the remotest areas soon after. Corruption exists in every field, whether it is police, business, education sector, politics, etc. To a large extent we are responsible for encouraging corrupt people to continue with their antics.

Similarly, when scams happen, it is not just people at the top level who are involved; rather it is a chain that follows. Corruption is a disease, which seeps into the entire system. It not only affects the economic system but the entire nation suffers.

## Analysis

| | |
|---|---|
| **Speaker 1:** | To the point, thought provoking and decent presentation. |
| **Speaker 2:** | Strong and logical arguments. |
| **Speaker 3:** | Shallow speech, lack of confidence. |
| **Speaker 4:** | Should have elaborated more instead of simply passing off. |
| **Speaker 5:** | Sums up the discussion with logical conclusion. |

## Winning Strategy

### Interpersonal Skills

It is reflected in the ability of the individual to interact with other members of the group in a brief situation. Emotional maturity and balance promotes good interpersonal relationships. The person has to be more people centric and less self-centered.

Example: To remain cool even when someone provokes you with personal comment, ability to remain objective, ability to empathize, non-threatening and more of a team player.

# SATYAM - A CASE OF FAILURE OF CORPORATE GOVERNANCE

## Do you think the Satyam scandal would impact Foreign Investments in India?

### Speaker 1

Yes, I completely agree that India is known as the IT capital of the world and a scandal of this kind tarnishes the reputation of the country to the hilt. When foreign investors will look at India for any investment, the Satyam scandal will always be there at the back of their minds. And since investments are about profits, trust has a major role to play. But after this Satyam scandal, investors' trust in Indian companies will not be the same. It will force investors to rethink about investing. However, apart from that it is not that foreign investments have not gained from other projects. Several other giant companies are continuing to make profits for themselves but are also helping the Indian economy. At this stage it is also important to remember that other countries are not completely free from corruption as well.

If we make a list of countries where corruption is high, India is on the 87th position, so we can say India is at a much better place than many other countries. Also, we must keep in mind that foreign investors when they decide to make an investment, they do not get influenced by one scandal it takes much more for them to go for a deal.

## Speaker 2

The Satyam scandal left a bad taste in everyone's mouth. A reputed IT company like Satyam to be involved in money laundering was unthinkable. What made the thing ugly was to know that the owners themselves were involved. This case was very similar to the Enron scandal. With thousands of employees' fate being uncertain, and thousands laid off, the entire picture was grim. Everybody involved with the company was assured that the worse is yet to come and it was better to wait patiently before all turns around again. The reputation that had taken years to build was shattered in a day. It was a matter of shame when the morning newspaper displayed the horror story of deceit. It was open for the world to see India's biggest IT fraud.

Satyam happens to be one of the major stake-holding companies in the market, and I am sure in due course it will bounce back. Also, now that Mahindra and Mahindra have taken over, and its entire top management reshuffled, it is only a matter of time when foreign investors will be back in business with Mahindra Satyam. According to FDI, it will continue to flow in no time, because, they could see through the statistics that even when Enron had gone through a scandal, it did not impact the economy much.

This is good news for everybody. I am sure foreign investors are not far away and the trust will soon be back. It is important to understand that investors are not so easily deterred by mere scandal; a lot goes into the matter before an investment is done.

## Speaker 3

Thank you my dear friends for your honest opinions. It is true that the chairman of Satyam, cooked up key financial results, including a fictitious cash balance of more than $1 billion. This act raised serious doubts about the IT revolution hype in India that attracted several international companies and significant foreign investments towards India.

The Wall Street Journal reported that B. Ramalinga Raju, founder and chairman of Satyam Computer Services Ltd., in his letter of resignation said that he exaggerated the profits for the past many years, overstated the amount of debt owed to the company, and understated its liabilities. Eventually, he said the scheme reached "simply unmanageable proportions" and he was left in a position that was "like riding a tiger, not knowing how to get off without being eaten."

But what cannot be ignored is during the time of Satyam revelations, the company's market valuation dipped by about 80% in merely 2 days India's Sensex index plunged 7.2%, as investors reassessed level of risk in the Indian market amid serious concerns about corporate governance and accounting standards across the Indian industry. Just as the saying goes, "one bad fish dirties the pond," similarly, it is true that the Satyam scandal brought great shame not just to our country but put a deep impact on our foreign investments. Though there are many IT companies in our country such as WIPRO, IBM, INFOSYS, TCS, etc., each company works hard to build a reputation which will attract foreign investors. Foreign investments are not profitable only for the concerned company but these investments also boost our economy.

However, instances of fraud and scams impact the Indian economy and foreign investments to an extent. There is no doubt that there will be investments but such irregularities makes the investees skeptical of their investments in our country.

## Speaker 4

I agree with many of our friends present here. I am also of the view that the Satyam scandal is not going to hurt our economy. I am also sure that a scandal cannot deter foreign investors from investing in Indian companies. The government is also very serious about dealing with these kinds of frauds and scams that impact the country's reputation. If we want to be on the global map as a business centre, we have to tackle these scams very seriously.

When the Satyam debacle happened, other Indian firms were deeply worried by the fall-out and tried to downplay it.

## Speaker 5

It is true that the Satyam scandal has brought shame and humiliation for our country, but it is better to stop living in the past and move forward. Out of hundreds of companies if one company is involved in fraudulent activities, it is best to take it as a bad experience and move forward, because there are still ninety-nine honest companies to do business with.

I do not disagree with the fact that the Satyam scandal created a negative impact on our reputation and forced the FII to rethink before investing in India. We should not forget that investors are looking for profits and even they are aware that one such incident does not affect the total credibility of a country.

Hong Kong based Political & Economic Risk Consultancy Ltd., had rated India (2009) as the riskiest of 14 Asian countries, not including Pakistan and Afghanistan. The Satyam scandal added additional risk if the Indian authorities and corporate sector fail to take adequate measures in order to restore the investors' confidence in India's publicly traded companies.

| | Analysis |
|---|---|
| Speaker 1: | Average speech. |
| Speaker 2: | Has a sound knowledge of the subject and places his points well. |
| Speaker 3: | Well-read, good knowledge of the scandal. |
| Speaker 4: | Does not disagree directly. Should have elaborated more. |
| Speaker 5: | Displays a positive attitude, is confident. |

## Winning Strategy

**Persuasive skills:**

The ability to analyze and persuade others to see the problem from multiple perspectives without hurting the group members.

**Example:** While appreciating someone else's point of view, you should be able to effectively communicate your view without overtly hurting the other person.

# Every cloud has a Silver Lining

## Speaker 1

What an interesting topic to begin a discussion on. I am a very optimistic person and I strongly believe in this saying. We are bound to meet with failure at some point of time in our life and there may be times when we are completely dejected. This is when we should have faith in ourselves and believe that good times are near. If the sky is cloudy and the day is dull...remember, "Every cloud has a silver lining'. This statement demonstrates the thought that whatever problem you may have at the present time will get sorted one day but you should not give up on the situation. Faith and belief in oneself is of prime importance. When problems arise, the inner strength in us gives us the power to go through it and work more effectively towards achieving a positive result. As the saying goes, "when gold is burnt repeatedly it shines more and becomes stronger".

## Speaker 2

My dear friends, we all know that failure is the pillar to success. I am sure there is no individual who has not failed in life. Even Sachin Tendulkar did not become a world-class cricketer overnight. He too had to struggle to reach where he is today. He has also scored ducks in his career. But that does not mean he became depressed and decided to quit the game. Rather he worked hard at the game and the rest is history.

### Speaker 3

I do not agree with the statement "Every cloud has a silver lining". Life is a constant struggle and unless you are born with a golden spoon, nothing comes easy. When we face problems in our work life, or personal life, many a times we become habitual of it and tend to accept life as a big problem.

### Speaker 4

My dear friends, I am sure we all know what an idiom is. "Every cloud has a silver lining" is also an idiom. It is commonly used to acknowledge the experience of a difficult time. When one says that every cloud has a silver lining, it is used as a form of encouragement. The thought behind it is that even dark clouds can have the sun peeking through creating a silver lining around the edges of the cloud. It is a comment on the human spirit and the desire to find meaning and purpose in all circumstances as well as the desire to be optimistic about the future.

### Speaker 5

No comments. My dear friends have already spoken about what I intended to say. I wish all my friends the very best in life. Thank you!

| | Analysis |
|---|---|
| **Speaker 1:** | A pleasant and confident start. |
| **Speaker 2:** | Just states an example and ends the discussion. |
| **Speaker 3:** | Disagrees strongly with the speakers. |
| **Speaker 4:** | Starts by explaining the idiom and raises good points. |
| **Speaker 5:** | Very unprofessional approach. Just sums up the argument without speaking much. |

## Winning Strategy

### Problem solving skills:

The ability to come out with divergent and offbeat solutions and use one's own creativity.

Example: While thinking of solutions, don't be afraid to think of novel solutions. This is a high-risk high-return strategy.

# Advertising is a Waste of Resources

## Speaker 1

I think, advertising is not a wastage of money because people, especially the youth, fall for what is shown or portrayed in advertisements. This makes the brand or the product popular and hence increases its sales. More sales lead to higher profits for the company.

However it is important that we remember that now-a-days almost all advertisements do not always depict the product as it originally is. This can be seen in the recent ad war between Tide and Rin washing powder. Tide claimed it contained real sandal and fragrance which was proved incorrect. We should always use our discretion while buying a product.

Ad companies design these advertisements in such a way that it easily catches the buyers' imagination. Thus, according to me advertisements are good till the time they are used to portray the product the way it is. We should be able to use our discretion as well and learn to differentiate between the good and the best. We know that every business organization wants long-term profit but in case of false advertisements it is just wastage of money.

## Speaker 2

I disagree with my dear friend because in my opinion advertising is not a waste of resources. This is till the time there is a limit to what is being spent. If a company has the funds to invest in advertisement to promote its product, then they should go for it. Advertisement is a form of marketing a product and is a long-term investment. Consumers are informed about new products, their unique features with the help of advertisement. There is cut-throat competition in the market to sell products. So companies want to reach out to more and more people. It is not always required to spend a mammoth amount on promoting a product. If the service or product is good or a little better than others, and is constantly innovating itself, then it is bound that customers will also cling or get drawn to it. Consumers want value for money and they know what is good and what is not. It would be foolish to think that an expensive and flowery advertisement can build customer loyalty if the basic product is not good.

There is no need to spend on continuous advertisements once the company has built rapport with the consumers. The product on its own will speak for itself. There is no replacement for quality. But it is equally important to promote a product through advertisements to reach out to customers in different corners.

## Speaker 3

In my opinion, advertising is definitely not a waste of money. Advertising plays an important role in modern society. It helps consumers make the right decision while buying goods and services. Today, advertisements are designed to draw the consumer's attention to products, for example when we want to buy mobile phones, popular movie stars endorsing the brand does impact our mind. Advertisements compete on price, brand value, look, and durability helping us find the cheapest or best value products. In most cases advertising does not make us go shopping – we would be planning to buy food, clothes, gifts, and entertainment anyway.

## Speaker 4

When a baby feels pain he cries, it is only then we come to know what he is feeling and what we should do for him; this is also a kind of advertisement done by the child. So unless the company who is going to launch the new product or a different variety of the existing products in the market advertises it how will we come to know about its features, the specialty, the options and choices of the particular product. A product will have the chance of being successful only when it has been promoted differently and should have some unique features in comparison to the existing products, and this can be conveyed to the common people only through advertisements through different modes.

## Speaker 5

What advertising does is to help us make better decisions on how to spend our money, by giving us more information about the choices available. So it is definitely not a waste of resources. Don't we love watching our favourite movie stars on TV. And yes, our choices do get influenced by advertisements.

## Analysis

| | |
|---|---|
| **Speaker 1:** | Starts of well but it becomes repetitive soon. |
| **Speaker 2:** | Stays away from building a team consensus/ disagrees with speaker 1. |
| **Speaker 3:** | Quite assertive, confident. |
| **Speaker 4:** | Draws an analogy and supports the argument. |
| **Speaker 5:** | Should have elaborated more on the points. |

## Winning Strategy

The ability to grasp the situation, take it from the day-to-day mundane problem level and apply it to a macro level.

**Example:** At the end of the discussion, you could probably summarize the findings in a few sentences that present the overall perspective.

# Commercialization of health care – Good or Bad?

**Speaker 1**

I will begin my speech by drawing everybody's attention towards today's time and age where commercialization has become an inevitable element. Healthcare has grown to become a productive sector for investment. Healthcare is no longer a luxury; it has become a necessity for every individual. So commercialization of healthcare has slowly made its presence felt. It is not a very happy situation where a man's basic need of good healthcare is now turned to be a lucrative business for doctors and hospitals.

Most people are of the opinion that doctors overcharge for their services and medical service has become highly commercialized. Non-commercialization occurs when a hospital reduces its charges and the doctors' fees for patients. This strategy has been followed by some of the biggest hospitals around the world and they have found success.

When hospitals present patients exorbitant bills for treatments, they are likely to lose potential customers from returning to the hospital. In addition, if the services rendered by the hospital are not up to the level, especially in comparison to the prices they demand, it impacts the reputation of the hospital in the long run. Hospitals with exorbitant prices may get patients only a select section of the society, i.e., the rich and creamy population, for a short- term. However, in the long-term it will lead to declining profits.

Whenever hospitals charge reasonably and provides quality services, it attracts more patients. This in turn leads to higher long-term profits. The only challenge in this situation is that the payback time of the project will be slightly longer in comparison to hospitals with hefty bills. This also creates a positive word of mouth in the market.

Many times hospitals that cater to high-end customers cannot compromise on the cost of service because of the luxury factor involved. The fact that the hospital provides deluxe services to high profile customers , who want high-end rooms and services, in addition to specialized doctors and treatment, will automatically lead to a large bill.

## Speaker 2

I agree completely with my dear friend. We all know that "health is wealth", but now this saying has been slightly modified to "wealthier is healthier". The chief reason for this new alteration could be the careless attitude of the government. It is the Department of Health's responsibility to ensure that they are able to provide good and clean and cost effective hospitalization and treatment to everyone at affordable prices. Unfortunately the government has not been able to do so. Treatment at government hospitals is not a pleasant experience any more. People are afraid of the kind of treatment and doctors provided by government hospitals. And when we look deeper it is corruption which majorly contributes to this.

Absence of good treatment at government hospitals has forced people to depend on the private hospitals for good treatment. It is important to keep in mind that one has to compromise on the money factor to get good healthcare facilities. Hospitals also invest a lot in medical equipments like scanning machines, X-Ray machines, chemicals for blood tests, urine tests, and so on. To meet these expenses private hospitals charge higher treatments.

Therefore, blaming all healthcare centers for commercialization is in appropriate. There are several hospitals that provide treatment to the poor, lower middle class families or the underprivileged, with help from various trusts and other human welfare institutions. There are many charitable hospitals that provide treatments absolutely free of cost.

## Speaker 3

My dear friends commercialization of healthcare is not acceptable at all. It gives a bad taste in the mouth thinking that hospitals can use medical help as a means to make money. For an individual food, health and education are his/her primary rights. However, there is a definite lack of primary facilities in this country. If critical facilities like healthcare is commercialized then survival of the common man can became a question. Keeping the monetary factor aside, we must remember that as a human being it is our social responsibility to respect and protect our fellow human beings.

## Speaker 4

Well friends, I think the issue of commercialization in healthcare is being confused with money laundering by the doctors. Commercialization of health care has bought about a sea of change in the health care sector. It would be foolish to imagine that if it were not for the equipment and treatment techniques introduced by the more innovative and mobile private sector health care institutions that our government would have in this short time improved government hospitals to whatever standard there is now.

One must realize that government negligence and indifference with which government doctors treat patients is equally to blame. Overlooking on part of the government towards these doctors reflects on their attitude towards their patients. If the government offered similar amenities to doctors and patients as in top private sector institutions then we could have expected similar treatment as well. The question that arises is – Would it be misleading to say that we would be looking at an ideal situation where the good is marked and the bad is done away with?

Food for thought friends!

## Speaker 5

My friends I do not agree that commercialization of health care is good. But in the society all types of health care centers are available and we have to decide as per our strength and economic stability.

## Analysis

| | |
|---|---|
| Speaker 1: | Sound knowledge, a good start. |
| Speaker 2: | Displays a positive attitude and agrees on speaker 1. |
| Speaker 3: | Limits himself to a paragraph but gives a precise and to the point argument. |
| Speaker 4: | Has some very good points to share. |
| Speaker 5: | Winds up the topic without speaking much. |

## Winning Strategy

The first implication is that the panel should notice you. Merely making a meaningful contribution and helping the group arrive at a consensus is not enough. You have to be seen by the evaluating panel to have made the meaningful contribution. What does that mean in practice?

# Are Indians less Quality Conscious?

## Speaker 1

It is wrong to say that Indians are not quality conscious. If we look at the lower income groups, who earn just enough to meet their basic needs, also reflect on the quality of the stuffs they purchase. Have we ever asked ourselves how we define quality! For low income groups, undiluted milk for their children is the best meal they can provide to their children. For middle income group people, anything that is well-processed works. And the elite class prefers eating and drinking the best.

When we withdraw money from ATMs or banks, we complain if the currency notes are soiled. And believe it or not, the local rickshawala who earns at the most Rs200 a day will refuse to accept a note that is soiled or torn. We often have a mindset that we can pass the torn notes to bus conductors or rickshawalas as they are happy to get money in whichever form. But sadly, this is not the case. The low income segment is the not always the one who compromises on quality.

Consider this, at every level of the social ladder; the best quality mark differs. While the quality consciousness factor is innate in every human being, it also depends on what they have in hand that decides what is best for them.

## Speaker 2

This statement holds true in certain cases as Indians can evaluate what is a good quality product. However, bad experiences in the past have damaged that opinion. In this competitive age Indians are not as competitive as the rest of the world. We tend to compromise many a times, however, the Western world introduced us to six sigma, to ensure minimum defects. This means that quality is extremely important. Six sigma and other quality standards are now accepted norms in most organizations as they have realized that quality matters for all.

## Speaker 3

Friends we all know that India is a democratic country, where people have the right to select the right leader to run the country. However, only 20% people think about the quality of potential leader they are voting for. 80% people are not bothered and are also not aware of the after effects of bad quality leader or product, and the benefits that are associated with best quality in respect to product or manpower.

## Speaker 4

Indians are less quality conscious and one reason for this is, to improve their skills they don't have good training like other countries have for their workers. They don't get good incentives for their work, which is another reason for their bad quality of work.

## Speaker 5

I think the problem is with the people of India who earn limited amount of money and are unable to afford expensive goods. Eventually, they compromise with the quality. There is one reason why the markets are fleeced with duplicate products which are of inferior quality. Also, competition is another reason why the average Indian seems to be less quality con-scious. The Indian markets are full of Chinese products which give stiff competition to Indian products. Chinese products are cheaper but are mostly inferior in quality.

| | Analysis |
|---|---|
| **Speaker 1:** | Assertive and smart points. |
| **Speaker 2:** | Confident, to the point and precise. |
| **Speaker 3:** | Starts with an example but deviates from the point altogether. |
| **Speaker 4:** | Poor content/deviates largely from the topic. |
| **Speaker 5:** | Talks about the Indian market and products. Sound knowledge of the topic. |

## Winning Strategy

You must ensure that the group listens to you. If the group listens, so will the evaluator. However, that does not mean that you shout at the top of your voice and get noticed for the wrong reasons.

# Advertising is all Glitter and Little Truth?

## Speaker 1

I completely agree with the topic. Advertisers often get movie or sports stars to promote a product. Unfortunately the celebrities promoting the product, most of the time, have no accountability. Endorsing a product necessarily does not mean using the product in his/her personal life. Advertisers have to depict what they think will appeal the customers, keeping in mind clients requirements. The core function of advertising is creating a need in the customer. As more and more products are launched the ads too increase. Glitter is a way to ensure brand recall, a very important factor for the advertising firms. Most often companies over showcase their product qualities, which becomes unfair.

For example, we see exaggerated ads on TV where a young man after chewing a particular gum becomes so cool that girls begin to follow him everywhere. Or take the example of a famous men's deodorant ad where after using that deodorant, girls chase him everywhere he passes by. In my opinion all this is totally misleading.

## Speaker 2

I agree with my dear friend that advertising firms carry the responsibility of giving customers unbiased information about products they are promoting. To reach a healthy bottom line, ad firms cannot shun their responsibility towards the society in general. Ad firms should develop and present content that are ethically created. This ethical mindset is often ignored by ad firms in their quest to ensure fair deals. There are several advertisements aired on TV and on billboards that show a disclaimer that the product is medically proven and it actually works.

## Speaker 3

Advertisements are made to catch the attention of the customers. Sometimes they might only glitter but sometimes they are also true. It all depends on what the client wants. Ad firms act on the instructions of their clients, so it would be wrong to blame them solely.

## Speaker 4

Advertising is a business and not charity. Companies hire advertisers for promoting their products and not vice versa. Fantastic advertisements take place when there is a fantastic product or service and the ad maker is able to attract the potential customers attention, and then leaves it on them to judge for themselves if they actually find the product or service worth buying. So in my opinion I think this discussion should end here.

## Speaker 5

Advertising is a booming industry and an important marketing strategy. It provides millions of jobs and contributes to the world economy. So there is partial truth in the statement. Some have compared advertisers to defense lawyers because they are expected to select the most inconsequential detail and weave an entire story around it. The whole concept lies in the ad maker's ability to portray the product slightly better than the competitors and get paid for it.

| | Analysis |
|---|---|
| Speaker 1: | A decent start. |
| Speaker 2: | Develops more on the points raised by speaker 1 and makes it interesting |
| Speaker 3: | Should have added more. Poor content. |
| Speaker 4: | Aggresive and vague. |
| Speaker 5: | Sums up well. |

## Winning Strategy

You have to be assertive. If you are not then, you will have to simply learn to be assertive for those 15 minutes. Remember, assertiveness does not mean being bull-headed or being arrogant.

# Film-makers are indulging in cinematic exploitation in the name of Folk Culture

## Speaker 1

This is an interesting topic. I am an avid movie buff. When a movie is played in a theater it is after the producer and director along with his actors have put their hard work together for us in reels. A movie is the end product of what the producer being the investor and the director the creator decide to create and produce and finally present before us. Now the intension behind the movie may vary from producer to producer. A producer and director may want to take the pulse of the movie goers and make a film that they think will be appreciated. It is a gamble to woo the crowd by showing what they want. There are filmmakers who want to capture the folk culture in their movie only to make money rather than making a film for a reason. This is cinematic exploitation in the name of folk culture and such film makers should be banned.

## Speaker 2

In my opinion, there are filmmakers who make movies to promote our values and culture to the world. If a movie is based on folk culture then it should expose the beauty of that culture and avoid any kind of 'masala' to lure the crowd. Folk culture must be preserved in its true form and should not be exploited for money, by depicting the same in movies and earning an Oscar nomination.

## Speaker 3

I think it is okay if filmmakers are making films with folk themes. However, one thing they should ensure is that the folk culture is portrayed with honesty and in such a way that people learn something from it. What I mean is that filmmakers should retain the natural beauty of the folk culture and avoid the adding commercial aspects to the movie.

## Speaker 4

I agree with this topic. The trend in movies is somewhat towards folk culture these days, which may soon fade away as the audience for such movies is very limited. Distributors can play these movies either in multiples where the intellectuals come to watch this kind of cinema or take it to the villages where the audience can relate to it. But due to the rage of winning International awards, more and more filmmakers are inclined to make such kind of movies. The challenge arises when unethical filmmakers exploit cultural themes for money or fame.

## Speaker 5

Honestly friends, I watch only Hollywood movies and have no interest in such kind of cinema. I am sorry but I do not have any valuable point to add. My dear friends have already spoken much about the issue.

| | Analysis |
|---|---|
| **Speaker 1:** | A pleasing and positive start. |
| **Speaker 2:** | Could have elaborated more. It was a decent start. |
| **Speaker 3:** | Repetitive. Nothing original. |
| **Speaker 4:** | Quite reasonable/confident |
| **Speaker 5:** | Stands alone. Doesn't try to build up a team consensus. |

## Winning Strategy

**Many participants often complain that they did not get a chance to speak. The fact is that in a Group Discussion no one is specially asked to speak. You have to start with a link and put your point across. It is unacceptable to keep one's mouth shut or just murmur which is inaudible, in a GD.**

# You can stop CORRUPTION

## Corruption is the main outcome of Democracy in India

### Speaker 1

Good morning friends! We live in a country which is infected with an incurable disease called corruption. Sadly our political system grants equality to everyone, and it gets easier to play around loopholes in the Indian Statute. It is true that democracy is not directly involved in promoting corruption but yes it does give power to the people. These corrupt people exploit their own country's resources for their own selfish gains. This is really sad that in a democratic system the country's adult population legally appoint the corrupt leaders, who in turn rob us. The fact that a democratic country like India is surrounded by corruption and directly or indirectly democracy is fuelling it.

### Speaker 2

My dear friend spoke very powerfully to prove his point but I have something different to say on this. Corruption is about personal equation and is dependent on an individual or organizations' personal value systems. Corruption is a price we pay for democracy. The two should not be interpret as a cause-effect relationship. Democracy gives choice to people to select the leaders on the basis of their capability and goodness. If people choose the wrong leaders then that is not a problem with democracy. It is a problem with the people as they are unable to exercise their powers.

## Speaker 3

Guys! Democracy does not support corruption at all. But the people themselves are greedy and selfish who are motivated by corruption. Corruption erupts from an individual's innate nature so why blame democracy.

## Speaker 4

When I compared the republic countries to democratic countries like India, Pakistan, etc., I discovered that the democratic nations have paved their own way in to corruption. In democratic countries the Prime Minster is the Head of State. In India, sadly our PM does not take any strict actions against corruption as it should. Corruption is a multi-layered disease which seeps in to different levels of people. Corruption begins at the grass root level and ends at the top most. This is why we have people like Anna who at an age of 70 + has to sit on a fast to curb corruption. The country's *aam janta* are all tired of the corrupt ministers and their scams. Democracy does not support corruption at all. It is the people's selfish motives that find an answer in corruption.

## Speaker 5

Whatever I wanted to say has already been spoken by my dear friends. I have nothing more to add to this except one point. I want to ask everyone a question. Do you think if India was not a democratic country then there would have been no traces of corruption? If corruption is the outcome of democracy then how is it that corruption in China is more than that in India. Moreover, corruption existed since time immemorial right, even during the time of the Mahabharata.

| | Analysis |
|---|---|
| **Speaker 1:** | Repetitive and vague. |
| **Speaker 2:** | Confident, to the point. Starts by praising speaker 1. |
| **Speaker 3:** | Very informal and unprofessional approach. |
| **Speaker 4:** | To the point, thought provoking and decent speech. |
| **Speaker 5:** | Sums up well by posing a question to all, but leaves his answer open-ended. |

## Winning Startegy

Participate in as many practice GD's as possible before you attend the actual GD. There is nothing like practice to help you overcome the fear of talking in a GD.

# Shortage of skilled Manpower in India

## Speaker 1

We say India is rich in resources; does that not include human resource? India has a vast resource of skilled manpower. MNCs outsource from India not only because of cheap labour but also because of certain other qualities like hard-working and committed people, clear accent that can be understood by all and many others. In India, every person is skilled at his job and only that person is able to complete it successfully. Had this not been true then we would not have had construction labourers for constructing our houses? And according to me, being master of one trade is better than being jack-of-all-trades and master of none.

## Speaker 2

Indians have ample manpower. We have very skilled and well-educated people in our country. But the problem is that the younger people do not make use of their skill and talent as much as possible. Instead of habits like reading books and playing, smoking and drinking have become the pastimes of teenagers. This has led to laziness among students.

## Speaker 3

Employers in India are struggling very hard to get talented candidates. This is also the outcome of our educational system. Out of 100 candidates only

15-20 candidates are skilled and those are also going to western countries and applying their skills there. They are working under white-collared people. Here one needs to remember that I am talking about only the present scenario and not about the past. In the old days (10-15yrs back), there is no doubt that Indians were more skilled than any other country.

## Speaker 4

In India, everybody compares our skills with people of other countries but nobody compares the population. The government is not backing students to improve their skills. Proper infrastructure is not being provided. 20% of the total population are highly skilled in India and the remaining (80%) are unskilled. If one looks at the statistics and enquires from the employers one can easily arrive at such conclusions.

## Speaker 5

Friends I am not criticizing any person in particular but the Indian political system administration and the government is responsible for the shortage of skilled manpower in India. I have recently read a survey in one of the reputed magazines that employers are not getting the right persons. 20% of the people are inventing new things by using their skills and the remaining 80% people are using their so-called skills in destruction of the existing things. This is very unfortunate. India has a huge population and also the infrastructure to train people in appropriate skills.

| | Analysis |
|---|---|
| **Speaker 1:** | Quite reasonable and healthy start. |
| **Speaker 2:** | Should have elaborated more/vague. |
| **Speaker 3:** | Strong argument, covers some good points. |
| **Speaker 4:** | Builds up the argument further by providing statistics. |
| **Speaker 5:** | Assertive and to the point. |

## Winning Strategy

An important implication is that making just any sort of contribution is not enough. Your contribution has to be meaningful. A meaningful contribution suggests that you have a good knowledge base. You are able to put forth your arguments logically and are a good communicator. The quality of what you said is more valuable than the quantity. There is this myth amongst many Group Discussion participants that the way to succeed in a Group Discussion is by speaking loudly and at great length. One could not be more wrong. You must have weight in your arguments.

Therefore, think things through carefully.

# In our economic matters, there is an excessive tendency towards Thinking rather than Doing

## Speaker 1

Friends I will open the discussion with my views which may be strong for some of you. Proper planning takes a longer time. However, when a long-term project is in question then it becomes obligatory to spend more time in the thought process so that the ideas evolves. Take the example of DMRC where all projects are complete prior to the timeline. India is making good progress in infrastructure development. The speed may not be very high but our duty is to help the process move efficiently rather than put blame on someone. India is the second fastest growing economy in the world; all that is needed is confidence in delivering instead of only relying on thinking about it.

## Speaker 2

In my opinion, India has no dearth of great thinkers. If we look at the list of famous inventors in different fields in the world, then the numbers of Indians are as many. The issue with us is that we invest a lot of time and effort in understanding things first and then comes implementation. In fact so much time goes into the thinking stage that at times implementation goes a little slower. This of course does happen in every field. If we look at how middle-class people are investing in share and stock broking and other financial investments. They have realized that it is an easy way of making good money. Yet there are less than 2% households in India who have actually invested in the stock market, in spite of heavy promotions and advertisements by financial companies. There are a number of people who know that our economy is booming and they know how and when to invest in the market. But they will not do so. Instead they will wait and watch. They are afraid to take risks. They will spend time thinking about it but will take baby steps when it comes to actions. So for our country to truly prosper this mindset has to change.

## Speaker 3

In my opinion the time taken to plan any policy or approach in India is so lengthy that by the time the policy or approach is executed, it loses its novelty and is no longer what the society needs. A recent example is the issue of the Jan Lokpal Bill. There is strong resistance for the Bill from the opposition ruling parties. This Bill apparently does not meet their requirements and hence they are extending no support to help pass the Bill in Rajya Sabha. The idea behind this is to show that they want a strong Lokpal Bill and on the other hand they are opposing the Bill. Endless discussions follow. In my view, what is needed at the moment is to first pass the Bill, amendments can be introduced at a later stage to make it a strong Lokpal Bill. I think this is a good example to drive home the point that not just in our economic matters but in all matters, there is an excessive tendency towards the thinking rather than doing.

## Speaker 4

Friends we all know that India is a very large and diverse country. We have both BPL and SEZ areas in our country. There are rich industrial areas and vast agricultural lands in another. Both contribute largely towards our economy. Because of the country's largeness it becomes difficult to develop an economic policy keeping in mind the different regions. This requires cautious planning to ensure that no one "feels" neglected. Any new policy takes time to be implemented as it has to follow a fixed pattern where it has to pass down from top to bottom in the governmental hierarchy. Yes, I strongly believe that our government has the ability to fasten the implementation process.

## Speaker 5

All that I want to say is that look at our politicians and their actions will say it all. Thank you. They only want to fill their pockets. Development is always planned and hardly executed. In India only thinking will not solve any problem. Instead the intention to do or complete the task is the solution. If we compare ourselves with our neighbour CHINA, it is evident that they are a much developed nation than us, in spite of a larger population. The reason is they not only think or plan but they also implement what they think or plan.

| | Analysis |
|---|---|
| **Speaker 1:** | Makes a reasonable start. |
| **Speaker 2:** | Quite researched and to the point. |
| **Speaker 3:** | Well aware of the burning issues/assertive. |
| **Speaker 4:** | A decent speech. |
| **Speaker 5:** | Impulsive but strong argument. |

## Winning Strategy

**Always enter the room with a piece of paper and a pen. In the initial two minutes write down as many ideas as you can.**

# Are MNCs superior to Indian Companies?

## Speaker 1

In my opinion, MNC's are definitely superior to Indian companies. Many MNCs have evolved on the Indian soil as a result of globalization and liberalization. This has resulted in stiff competition that the domestic industrial sector is facing from them. There is no doubt that MNCs have brought improved products and services along with efficiency. However, when we look at the Indian companies in comparison to the MNCs, we realize that Indian companies have a long way to go before they are with par. There are instances when during job placements, a candidate after having gone through the interview process in many companies, finally is offered similar positions in two companies. One is an Indian company and the other an MNC. The candidate automatically prefers to accept the offer of the MNC because he knows that in an MNC he will be offered a better pay package, better benefits and facilities and a healthy work environment. He may also get an opportunity to work overseas, if he performs well in his present organization. So there is a sense of security in the mind of the candidate who joins an MNC. However, Indian companies are not bad either. To match up to MNCs they too are raising their pace, and can even match up provided they change the way they function.

## Speaker 2

In my opinion competition enhances the quality of products or services. Organization that produce customer oriented products and also ensures after sales services are successful in boosting their productivity and sales and also manages to maintain their position in such stiff competition as well. So who benefits in this entire game of the best is the consumer. As a consumer myself, I can vouch that both MNCs and Indian companies are good, as long as they do not compromise on the product and service they provide. From an employee's point of view, an MNC could be superior depending on better infrastructural facilities, better standard of living, higher salary and global career opportunity, but Indian organizations too are matching up to MNCs. They too provide better salaries and benefits. So it is incorrect to keep a bias in our minds that MNC are better than our Indian companies.

## Speaker 3

In my view MNCs are superior to Indian companies when it comes to better work culture, growth, increase in employment, development in industrial sector, etc. Some even help farmers with better technology and facilities to improve their agricultural produce. However, it is not that Indian companies are any less than MNCs. Indian companies are also in the hunt now. They are also fast reaching higher growth and providing better work benefits. In the near future Indian companies will also reach the status of MNCs. And some Indian brands will become multinationals in the near future.

## Speaker 4

I disagree with my dear friends who underestimate our Indian companies. I would like to bring to your notice that several Indian companies are recognized all over the world for we have some great entrepreneurs as well. MNCs have proved to be a boon for India as they introduced India to the global market. In my opinion, Indian companies are indeed superior because we know our human resources as well as other resources better than the MNCs. Being Indians we know what our customers want; hence we have products that meet specific needs. In fact, we should encourage using products from Indian companies as this will help our country prosper.

## Speaker 5

I would like to bring an important fact about MNCs. MNCs such as Coca Cola, Pepsi, Mountain Dew, Mc Donald's all have a strong customer base in India. These brands may have initially faced criticism on their quality and pricing, however, with proper planning and strategies they managed to overcome the obstacles and what's more, people continue to consume these products. These products also have a foothold even in villages. But when we rack our minds to recall the name of an Indian soft drink brand, we are left wondering. This only manages to prove that in terms of marketing, promotion, publicity and crisis management MNC's are way better.

## Analysis

| | |
|---|---|
| **Speaker 1:** | Draws a good comparison. |
| **Speaker 2:** | Provides a detailed, thoughtful analysis. |
| **Speaker 3:** | Very average, nothing new to add. |
| **Speaker 4:** | Decent presentation. |
| **Speaker 5:** | Well researched and sums up well. |

## Winning Strategy

If you are asked to speak on a topic where you are expected to take a stand, say for example, "Should India sign the comprehensive Test Ban Treaty?" Note down the points form both sides of the argument. It will be useful on two counts:

First, if you do not start the GD and are not amongst the first five speakers and find that everyone in the group is talking for the topic, then it makes sense to take the alternate approach and oppose the topic even if you initially intended to talk for the topic.

Second, it helps to have knowledge of how group members who take a stand diametrically opposite to yours will put forth their argument and to be prepared with counter arguments.

# Is it fair for banks to use Force to recover Loans?

## Speaker 1

Well this is an interesting topic. I have seen several banks resorting to third party collection process to get back their money. But in my opinion banks have no right to use force on the defaulting customer. Whenever banks give out loans to customers they take collateral which is more or less the same amount they are lending to the customer. The collateral could be in the form of insurance policies or deposits, so that the bank always has the choice to take possession of the defaulter's assets and recover the money. And if the bank fails to verify the customers' credibility while loan sanctioning, then it is the bank's fault completely. The bank should check all details and conduct thorough background checks if they want to avoid any kind of defaults. In case of lapses the bank should not harass the customer. It is the bank's fault and the customer should not be made to suffer at the hands of goons.

## Speaker 2

When we all apply for a loan, banks always check the customer's credit history. But banks perform their duty in a proper way. I have a friend who works in the bank collection department and he has seen many people who take loans simply to default. I don't know what is the problem with customers, when they need finance, they walk up to the banks and when the banks need their money returned they simply skip. I don't know why they don't ask for help from their relatives and only approach the bank. Some customers complain that sales executives keep on calling to provide them with loans. But if you have ever travelled in trains, buses, etc there are lots of small sellers who try to convince us to purchase their product, but we only purchase if we need it, otherwise we ignore it. To conclude, if banks are providing loans to customers when they really need them, then what is the problem with the customers paying these back?

## Speaker 3

I accept the fact that some amount of fault lies with the bank. But are the people correct in what they are doing. If you know that you will not be able to pay the amount back why do you have to get the loan. In cases where something backfires unexpectedly I can understand but there are people who deliberately get loans and avoid paying them back and the bank has to take some steps as money is at stake. So the fault lies with both parties I'll say. The bank should act responsibly while giving loans and so should citizens while applying for loans.

## Speaker 4

Banks these days are selling loans like vegetables to feed the profit hungry shareholders and then using all kind of tactics like sending goons to recover the money. This is not acceptable to any society. India is a country where nearly 40% of the people are living in extreme poverty and the other 25% are just above the poverty line. They will accept any kind of loan without even considering its terms and conditions. My point is the banks must ensure the repayment capacity without exception before approving loans. This is also critical to the reputation of not just banks but the whole financial system.

## Speaker 5

In my opinion, if banks always help customer in every circumstances, customers should also be honest in returning the money they have taken in need. But customers will be customers and their mindset is to default, customers have the money to pay mobile bills, electricity bills, school fees, vehicle fuel, etc, then why not for loans?

| | Analysis |
|---|---|
| Speaker 1: | Very aggresive, sounds unfriendly. |
| Speaker 2: | Comes up with some good examples.decent presentation. |
| Speaker 3: | Repetitive/average. |
| Speaker 4: | To the point and precise. |
| Speaker 5: | Vague/does not talk much. |

## Winning Strategy

Everybody else will state the obvious. So highlight some points that are not obvious. The different perspectives that you bring to the group will be highly appreciated by the panel. Some pointers on being relevant while having a different perspective are:

Be careful that the "something different" you state is still relevant to the topic being debated.

Can you take the group ahead if it is stuck at one point?

Can you take it in a fresh and more relevant direction?

# Should India break Diplomatic Ties with Pakistan?

## Speaker 1

I strongly believe that Pakistan is not in favour of peace with India since it is behind the proxy war since 1990. In my opinion, if a war breaks out between the two countries, India has more to lose in comparison to Pakistan. Our neighbour Pakistan has to deal with a number of social problems such as, poverty, education, and unemployment. It has not achieved the kind of economic growth that India has. I feel probably Pakistan is resentful of India's prosperity and hence want to create hindrance in the form of terrorism to bar India's peace processes.

India should detach itself from all the ties it has with Pakistan. Trade, culture everything. But that would affect the gas pipelines coming from Iran via Pakistan. The matter is crucial and should be handled tactfully.

## Speaker 2

There's a saying, "Ghosts of kicks, don't understand words". History reminds us of "Pearl Harbor" , a landmark event in the US, that was destroyed by the Japanese. To combat this attack by the Japanese, the Americans dropped the atom bomb and destroyed Hiroshima and Nagasaki. Again, we all know of the attacks on the twin World Towers in the US by the terrorists which led to large scale destruction in Afghanistan. Americans believe in "a spade for a spade, an eye for an eye". That is the reason why America is still considered a super power, in spite of fighting recession. Friends, I would like to point out that giving back does not mean misusing power rather it asserts to the world of its dignity. I suggest that India in spite of so many terrorist attacks and continuous disagreements with Pakistan, should go ahead and severe all diplomatic ties with Pakistan. This will ensure that Pakistan also gets a message that we are no longer interested in peace talks, because there is no point in one-sided peace talks.

## Speaker 3

I would like to begin with the famous statement that our Prime Minister Dr Manmohan Singh made on our relationship with our neighbours, i.e., "We can change our friends but we cannot change our neighbours". If I gaze at all our interesting and challenging neighbours, it is evident that India shares lukewarm relations with all its neighbours. So we may end up asking ourselves if India has any problems with her diplomatic policies. Coming to the point I would say that India must engage herself into a diplomatic process with Pakistan because breaking diplomatic ties with Pakistan will not realize any of India's objectives. Instead, India must use its economic muscles and international relations to pressurize Pakistan to fight terrorism at its end.

## Speaker 4

I am completely against the idea of India breaking all diplomatic ties with Pakistan. Pakistan is home to several terrorist groups and if India breaks all ties with her then Pakistan will get a chance to wage war against us again. And as my dear friend has already said war will not impact Pakistan as much as it will impact India. India has lots to lose economically in case of a war. Also if Pakistan bond with China, our closest neighbour, then the impact will be worse than what we can anticipate. So politically and economically, India should continue with her diplomatic relations as it will also portray to the world who is the real culprit.

## Speaker 5

If at any point of time India contemplates breaking diplomatic ties with Pakistan it should first update her defense system with latest weaponry. The reason is that our politically unstable neighbour is prone to be taken over by extremists or the ISI or even its own army.

## Analysis

| | |
|---|---|
| **Speaker 1:** | Confident and mature start. |
| **Speaker 2:** | Aggressive and well-researched. |
| **Speaker 3:** | Average, does not add much to the argument. |
| **Speaker 4:** | Raises some new points and adds another dimension. |
| **Speaker 5:** | Starts off well but ends up soon. |

## Winning Strategy

Always attempt to build a consensus.

Nobody expects a group of five or ten intelligent, assertive people, all with different points of view on a controversial subject to actually achieve a consensus. However, what matters is "did you make attempts to build a consensus?"

The reason why an attempt to build a consensus is important is because in most work situations you will have to work with people in a team, accept joint responsibilities and take decisions as a group.

You must demonstrate the fact that you are capable and inclined to work as part of a team.

# Should important services like transport be left to Market Forces?

## Speaker 1

In my opinion important services like transport should not be left to market forces. Transportation facilities are essential for optimum growth. For instance, the expansion plan of any city will not get realized if the government does not create new transport facilities. In case the government is slack in its initiative of creating better transportation facilities, the common people will face difficulties and this will obstruct growth.

## Speaker 2

Actually if you leave the important and basic services such as transport to market forces they will only focus on the areas from where they can actually make a buck like the cities and towns, but as almost 60% of the Indian population lives in rural areas what about them? Don't they have equal right to transport facilities? So if the complete public transport will be left to private players I guess a majority of our population will be devoid of it completely.

## Speaker 3

Dear friends, good transport facilities is an ardent need of a developing country like India as most of the people still live in villages and also about 50% people are below poverty line so they can't afford to buy a vehicle. If the transport facilities are good it will reduce the necessity to buy a vehicle and people will also be able to travel comfortably.

Also, if you look at what E.Sridharan has done for the Delhi public commuters you will be startled. His contribution towards Delhi Metro is commendable. He has been able to cut travel time phenomenally. But to top it all, is the fact that the Delhi Metro has also helped to make commutation easier and better.

## Speaker 4

I do not wish to speak much on this subject as it does not interest me. However, important services such as transportation should remain only with the government because private sector forces work only for profits and has no interest to contribute towards public betterment. When a comparison between government and market forces is drawn, the differentiator is quality. If there is competition between two or more players then the situation may turn out to be different and the quality of services may also improve. So probably we should come up with public-private type of entity to gain benefit from both worlds.

## Speaker 5

In my view if the important services are handed over to the private agencies, they will charge exorbitant amounts. It is important to create adequate policies to avoid exploitation by the private companies. I think if we leave important and basic services such as transport to market forces they will only focus on the areas from where they can actually make a buck like the cities and towns. But unfortunately almost 60% of the Indian population lives in rural areas. Don't you think they have equal rights to have transport facilities? So if the complete public transportation is left to private players, then a majority of the population will be devoid of it completely.

| Analysis | |
|---|---|
| **Speaker 1:** | Starts up with some good points but does not elaborate. |
| **Speaker 2:** | Poses good questions, confident. |
| **Speaker 3:** | Sound knowledge of the subject, decent arguments. |
| **Speaker 4:** | Does not flatly deny to speak. Ultimately makes his point. |
| **Speaker 5:** | Average speech. Repetitive. |

## Winning Strategy

A Group Discussion is your chance to be vocal. The evaluator wants to hear you speak. Be as natural as possible. Do not try and be someone you are not. Be yourself.

# Developing countries need trade, Not Aid

## Speaker 1

I completely agree that developing countries need trade rather than aid because aid will only fulfill the short-term needs and demands of a country. And this is not really a situation a country can rely on. Aid can be granted for a specific time after which the country has to find ways and means to internally grow and develop. This can happen only with the help of trade which will increase productivity and in turn the growth of the nation. For a nation's development, it is essential to have capital and this capital will come from trade.

## Speaker 2

I consider aid and trade to be similar to the debt equity ratio. Here trade is first and aid is second. In a country like ours where we have a booming economy, yet there are times when the country is hit by a natural disaster like an earthquake or a Tsunami. It is when there is need of aid. Several poor countries such as Somalia, Bangladesh, and Haiti receive huge amount of foreign aid to fight poverty and a huge population. In fact in times of need India also provides aid to disaster struck other countries. However, in developing countries like India overseas trade is increasing by the day and trade deficit is slowly heading towards negligible. There is a lot of growth opportunity in our nation so we must be patient and stay positive

## Speaker 3

Being a part of a developing country I am proud to say that we need trade and not aid from the super powers. We know we have the potential to become a developed country. We have manpower and we have intellect. But as an irony we also do have poverty. Therefore, I will say that we do need aid, of course just to a certain extent. But the thing we really need is full-fledged trade. Because that can make us independent!

## Speaker 4

Hello friends! I agree with speaker 1 when he said that developing countries definitely need trade and not aid. I believe that for any developing country to prosper, it should exchange trade with neighbouring and other developed countries. Export and import is a key way to trade with other countries. This helps in improving the economic conditions and it develops a good bond between them. In fact, trade within the country is equally crucial for a country's growth. One cannot always survive on aid, he should be given an opportunity to work and grow. Similarly, developing countries who are trying to grow and develop and reach where developed countries like USA, UK are, then it has to work on improving its trade structure and accept aid only in times of calamities.

## Speaker 5

I'm very glad to speak about this topic. In my view developing countries always need trade for their development. Aid makes countries find temporary solution to their problems, but trade makes countries solve their problems permanently. Trade increases the economic condition of the country. In the era of globalization, trade helps to exchange our goods and services with other countries and this way we get to familiarize ourselves with the culture of other countries and slowly we learn to adopt the good things from the other country into our culture.

| | Analysis |
|---|---|
| **Speaker 1:** | A decent start. Should have elaborated more. |
| **Speaker 2:** | Sound knowledge of the subject/clever points. |
| **Speaker 3:** | Though precise but forceful. |
| **Speaker 4:** | Tries to build up a team consensus |
| **Speaker 5:** | Average summing up. |

## Winning Strategy

Opening the discussion is not the only way of gaining attention and recognition. If you do not give valuable insights during the discussion, all your efforts of initiating the discussion will be in vain.

Your body language says a lot about you — your gestures and mannerisms are more likely to project your attitude than what you say.

●●

# SECTION 2

The topics discussed in this section pertain to common General Knowledge Topics and are commonly seen as GD topics in various competitive examinations, i.e. CAT, MAT, IIMs, BPOs, Bank PO and many other qualifying examinations.

1. Marriage and beyond
2. Communicate to stay happily married
3. Infertility
4. Internet – need or curse
5. Is Philosophy just arm chair theory?
6. Success is all about human relations
7. Censorship is the need of the hour
8. Education and success– is there a correlation?
9. We don't learn from history, we repeat it
10. If there were no armies in the world......
11. Wisdom does not come with age
12. Management education–Is it necessary to succeed in business
13. The changing role of women in India
14. NGOs – role in bringing development
15. IPL
16. Semesters system…. boon or curse?
17. Superstitions
18. Bigamy
19. Kids today are not what they used to be
20. Examinations - has it killed education?
21. Are beauty pageants necessary?
22. Terrorism
23. Impact of television reality shows on children
24. Sex education
25. Inflation
26. Surrogacy
27. AIDS
28. Facebook
29. Twitter
30. Anna and Jan Lokpal Bill
31. FDI in Retail in India
32. Workplace problems that women employees face
33. Wrongful Termination Lawyers: Angels in Shinning Armours
34. Bankruptcy – A Lifeline for Debtors
35. SEO....The New Tool to Enhance Your Website
36. Depression: a common Ailment among youth
37. Indian Hockey – Near Extinction

# Marriage and Beyond

Marriage is a special event in the lives of two individuals who decide to share their joys and sorrows for the rest of their lives. Taking marriage vows is an important ritual in any marriage ceremony, irrespective of creed or religion. Marriage vows refer to the solemn promises the betrothed couple makes to each other in the presence of guests and the priest. This tradition is an integral part of any marriage ceremony. It sets the right tone to a relationship, which is supposed to be happy and long lasting. The vows one takes at the wedding ceremony must reflect one's honest feelings for their beloved. The words uttered, have been included as part of the wedding ceremony after been chosen carefully and without any trace of ambiguity. The sacredness of Hindu wedding vows reflects 6000 years of culture and heritage. Hinduism is one of the largest religions in the world. Myriads of customs and religions have merged into this polytheistic religion to give it a unique charm of its own. Hindu wedding vows are replete with a deeply religious connotation in which the divine aspects of marriage are highlighted.

Hindu marriage vows allude to various stages of married life. Although Hindu marriage vows differ slightly in comparison to other religion, the core values more or less remain the same. A Hindu marriage vow is taken while the couple is instructed to undertake the *Saat Phere* or the sacred seven steps. Each step is symbolic of the forward motion of life, along with the partner.

In today's world marriage is slowly losing its grip. If we look at the modern day divorce trends, what strikes one first is that education, wealth, commitment, and smartness have nothing to do with what leads to eventual separation or divorce.

This is both confounding and scary. In fact, most singles shy away from marriage only for the fear of making a wrong choice, which might end up in a messy and heartbreaking divorce. When one realizes that none of the above mentioned things are a factor or play a role in preventing the marriage from becoming a mere divorce statistic, one can see that things start to go wrong at the beginning of the relationship itself. In fact it begins with the so-called chemistry the couple thinks they have

Majority of couples, when asked by parents why they have chosen each other, say that it is mainly because of the amazing chemistry between them. In most cases, this chemistry subconsciously has to do with physical appearances and sexual attraction. The sad part is that it takes hardly six months for this so-called chemistry to evaporate, unless the foundation is strengthened by other compatibility factors. When the chemistry no longer plays a role in sustaining the marriage, the affected couples try to work extra hard on the marriage out of guilt feelings when they discover that the attraction towards the partner has waned. Pity, kindness, or simply obligation takes over and the marriage limps on without any real bonding or love between the couple.

Marriage is regarded as above of all human relationships and should never be taken lightly. Marriage is far more profound than our contemporary culture makes us believe. It is a life-long commitment that restrains self-centeredness, self-indulgence and self-gratification. It is the one relationship that effectively prepares and conditions us.

# Communicate to stay Happily Married

Society today has undergone tremendous change and this is mainly due to the work ethics that demand long and committed work hours with little time for family and relaxation. In a family, if the wife is unemployed and simply waits endlessly for the husband to come home and relieve her of her boredom, it leads to major complexities. Complexities in marriage are on the upswing with both partners having to do a complete analysis of each other's needs and trying to meet demands at least halfway. Tremendous willpower is the need of the day and unless there is a holistic approach, divorce and unhappiness will soon take over.

It is often said, when a movie has unprecedented success, it is all about the casting. It is the initial decision that has to be taken very carefully as that is when the fate of a marriage is usually decided. Make your choice wisely; give it serious thought, weigh the pros and cons well before zeroing in on your mate as it is the one decision that is going to make or break your marriage. Any follow-up action like trying to save a failing marriage will usually be futile and any idea that one can actually make a marriage work rarely works out. Societal pressures may make a couple hesitate to take the final step and they may try to continue in an empty relationship that in no way tackles the root of the problem.

So if one is on the threshold of a relationship, he/she must check it out from all points before deciding on marriage. They must take into account factors other than magical chemistry; check out comfort and compatibility levels before they decide that this relationship is for the long haul.

Whether it is an arranged marriage or a love marriage, a girl and boy have to consider certain basic issues which will go a long way in ensuring that they have made a right choice of life-partner. It is true that opposites do attract, but it is also true that the marriages that work best are with couples that share similar values, beliefs, and interests. This is not as if you have to select a carbon copy of yourself! Surely nothing can be more tedious or boring – after all, how many of us would want to marry a similar person? Marrying a mate who will probably work towards achieving the same goals and who has the same values in life will certainly go a long way in keeping the marriage intact. Having different interests is also a big plus point in any marriage. Sure, it is wonderful to spend a lot of time together – but all your time? And also, it will do you good to remember that it is the quality of time spent together and not the quantity that really counts. There are many couples that simply enjoy being together day and night and who love to do things together. Even for such inseparables, some time apart is good as it gives you a fresh outlook on your lives, not to mention giving you both something new to talk about, something that is separate from your daily lives and interests.

Of course, it goes without saying that communication is probably at the top of the list on the compatibility issue. Being able to discuss dreams, goals and what's in your heart is very important, as well as having someone who will listen closely to what you say and having some empathy as to how you feel. That's not to say that your partner wants to hear constant complaints about one thing or another. Yes, we all need "a shoulder to cry on" occasionally; just don't make a habit of it. So, is your man/woman the right material for all this? Are you able to share your thoughts without inhibitions?

Discussing issues like where one will be staying, whether in-laws are going to be part of one's lives, how soon and how many children one's planning to have, whether career is going to play an important part in the general scheme of things – these are a few basic issues that need to be discussed before one takes the plunge. Intimacy is also a very important part of keeping a marriage alive and happy. And intimacy doesn't mean just sex. Being close, holding hands, relaxing with each other, speaking of one's hopes and dreams of the future, helps to build a close relationship, and win the trust of one's partner.

Are you able then to totally relax in your chosen one's company? Are you able to discuss freely anything under the sun and find solutions to problems by just opening up to your partner? Is there enough empathy on both sides? If so, go ahead and just set the date – your journey together is sure to be a fruitful one and happy days are surely ahead!

# Infertility

Infertility primarily refers to the biological inability of a person to contribute to conception. Infertility may also refer to the state of a woman who is unable to carry a pregnancy to full term. There are many biological causes of infertility, some which may be bypassed with medical intervention. Women who are fertile experience a natural period of fertility before and during ovulation, and they are naturally infertile during the rest of the menstrual cycle. Fertility awareness methods are used to discern when these changes occur by tracking changes in cervical mucus or basal body temperature.

One definition of infertility that is frequently used by reproductive endocrinologists, the doctors specializing in infertility, to consider a couple eligible for treatment if:

- A woman under 35 has not conceived after 12 months of contraceptive-free intercourse. Twelve months is the lower reference limit for Time to Pregnancy (TTP) by the World Health Organization.
- A woman over 35 has not conceived after 6 months of contraceptive-free sexual intercourse.

The idea is that for women beyond age 35, every month counts and if made to wait another six months to prove the necessity of medical intervention, the problem could become worse. The corollary to this is that by definition, failure to conceive in women under 35, isn't regarded with the same urgency as it is in those over 35.

Alternatively, the NICE guidelines define infertility as failure to conceive after regular unprotected sexual intercourse for two years in the absence of known reproductive pathology. A couple that has tried unsuccessfully to have a child after a certain period of time is sometimes said to be subfertile, meaning less fertile than a typical couple. Both infertility and subfertility are defined as the inability to conceive after a certain period of time (the length of which vary), so often the two terms overlap.

If both partners are young and healthy and have been trying to conceive for 12 months to one year without success, a visit to the family doctor could help to highlight potential medical problems earlier rather than later. The doctor may also be able to suggest lifestyle changes to increase the chances of conceiving. Women over the age of 35 should see their family doctor after six months as fertility tests can take some time to complete, and age may affect the treatment options that are open in that case.

A family doctor will take a medical history and give a physical examination. They can also carry out some basic tests on both partners to see if there is an identifiable reason for not having achieved a pregnancy yet. If necessary, they can refer patients to a fertility clinic or a local hospital for more specialized tests. The results of these tests will help determine the best fertility treatment.

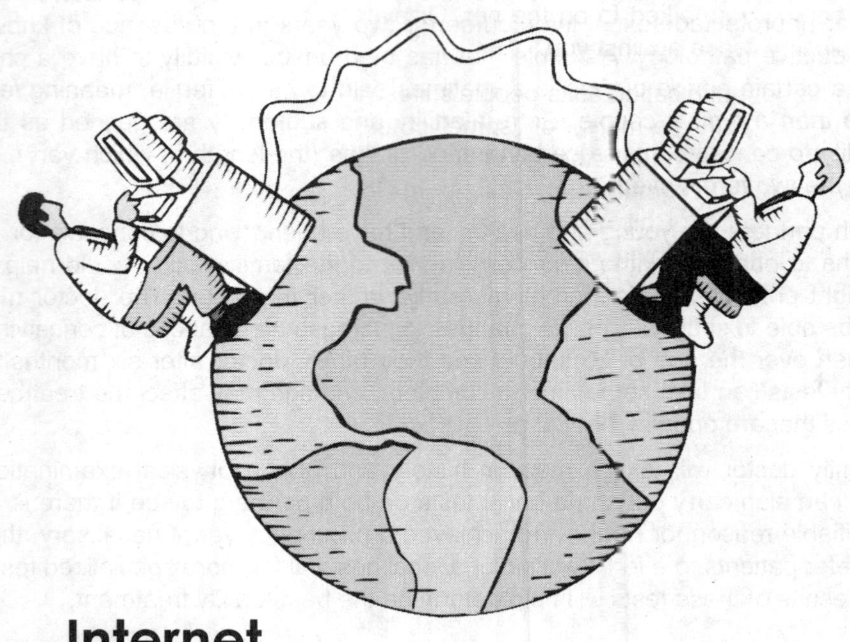

# Internet – Need or Curse?

We live in the age of information. The latest technologies develop every day and even every minute. Now we can find someone we are looking for in a very short time using e-mail, mobile technologies, paging system and others. There are no inaccessible places in the world, so the distances now seem not so big as they looked hundred years ago. The most important way of communication nowadays is the Internet. It started in 1960 when some governmental organizations in the US wanted to connect their systems in a very reliable net that couldn't be affected by war. Later this was developed further and now we have a big computer network all over the world. Nowadays people use the Internet for everything, for casual work like buying food, reading books, talking to friends. Customers discover that they can send messages to more than 30 million people all over the world and hold conferences about anything they want to. It improves the communication process and makes it easier.

On the other hand, there are some negative aspects of the Internet. Crime has been a growing problem all over the world for the last 30 years and now, it seems like there is no better place like the Internet to cheat. Everyone has tried different chat portals. There you can meet your old friends, or on the contrary, make some new ones. Suddenly, people don't even notice how they start to rely on new friends and believe whatever they say. Not just this, it could be a lot worse if you decide to meet these people in reality, because they might not be what you expected to see. Your virtual friend could turn out to be absolutely different from the person you talked to on the net. Or even worse, he could hurt you or use physical violence against you.

Remote communication suits people's lifestyles. People get used to discussing everything using e-mails, or some other message sending system, but, sometimes, they would rather go down to the pub or a restaurant, because some problems are too complicated to explain in virtual reality, especially if they involve facts and figures. Children also use the net to play games or to communicate with friends. Everything would be alright if there were only websites with decent content. Unfortunately this is not the case. There are millions of websites with pornography, cruelty, vice etc. It harms children's minds; it's bad for children's individual development. Nobody can deny that children are very curious. The net proposes virtual reality shops, where people can buy everything they want to. But, if children surf the net without adults being around, who would stop them from ordering some things or facilities from shops like that? It could be a real challenge for all family budgets.

In conclusion, the first step to make you and your children safe when you are surfing the net is to know about all the dangers and then trying to avoid them. It is essential to speak about problems like this because the net is not only a good implement to improve our knowledge and to communicate with people, it is also a big part of our everyday life. All we have to do is use it for the right purposes.

# Is Philosophy just an Armchair Theory?

The big question in this topic is philosophy just an armchair theory or in any way useful to our day-to-day life? We can just relax and reap the benefits of philosophy, by following some simple principles in life. First, let us learn to accept whatever comes and do only the right things in life to make life happier. We will come more close to philosophical life by shredding our ego. The state of mind where we accept anything and sacrifice anything is called philosophical life. We have studied that Lord Rama's expression did not change when he was told that though he will be the king initially, afterwards, he has to leave the kingdom to his brother Bharatha and live in the forest.

Be a self-critic, analyze yourself, correct yourself and walk in the correct path. To err is human; so don't find fault with others, if something goes wrong. If any negative thoughts come into your mind about anything or anybody, try to get such thoughts out from the mind and fill the mind with positive thoughts. Even if somebody does some harm to you, think about any good deed done by them for you or for somebody else. In this way hatred will ooze away from the mind. Armchair pursuit of philosophy is not at all required.

Philosophy is not a dry subject. It can be practiced easily. You need not put all the blame on fate, if something goes wrong. Accept the failure and try to make it a success. You have to accept all the feelings, which generate in your mind like happiness, sorrow, anger, irritation, peace, frustration etc. You need not control your thoughts. React to good feelings only and push the bad feelings deep inside the mind. If a sudden change comes in your daily life like a transfer, accept it, because it may be good for your future. If you happen to hurt anybody, knowingly or unknowingly, say sorry and take redressal action immediately. One does not degrade oneself by accepting to any wrong act. By correcting yourself, your reputation will increase. Don't develop the feelings of hatred or revenge for somebody who does harm to you. Don't waste your precious time; just move away from the situation and forget it. Philosophy is the right approach with positive mental attitude.

You must live in the present all the time. Don't think about the bad things that have happened in your life in the past. Day dreaming about the future also will not help you in your present life. Learn the lessons from the past, live in the present, and make future plans. Enjoy all the fun in life. Be happy and make others happy. Self-surrender and orders of discipline are the methods of applying philosophy in daily life. Every day, while getting up say to yourselves that today is most important and that you will do all the good things in life that day. This is the perfect way to spend your days.

There is a famous saying, "Better to light a small candle than to curse the darkness." You must not expect others to do a good thing. You yourself can start the process. The Bhagavat Gita says that whatever has already happened is good and whatever is to come will also be good. So, always think about good things only. Real philosophical view lies in learning about moral responsibility and intentional action. You should learn to balance the emotional response and reasoning about everything. In tough situations, you should see the problems, put yourself in the shoes of the affected person and take unbiased decisions. It can be concluded that philosophy is not just an armchair theory, but can be practiced in day-to-day life for attaining success in all walks of life.

●●

# Success is all about Human Relations

Someone once said, "At the end of your life when you are old, fragile, perhaps sitting in a wheelchair, nursing home, or on life support, what will be important to you?"

Success is the unconditional love you feel for the individuals that surround you. If you take time out to be with friends, help your neighbours, bond with your family and relatives, then also take the time out to ask your maid or newspaper boy how their day has been. When you are at the last moments of your life and you are surrounded by people you love – that is when you will experience the warmth from others. This is when you will have truly succeeded.

Getting success through relations and contacts is not success. Think about a person who comes from an under-privileged background and reaches the heights of success. Abraham Lincoln is just one example of true success. Pele, the greatest football player, did not succeed on the basis of human relations. To maintain relations is a very good thing, but to use the relations as a ladder to success is very bad. The modern world is so bad; it has changed the definition of success to exploring the world and knowing the people around you.

Success comes from within. If you're happy with the way you live your life and you haven't hurt anybody in the process then you can regard yourself as being a success. To me, success means happiness, contentment and having warmth of relationships. In today's context success means having lots of materialistic gains but these will provide satisfaction for a short period only. In the long run, relationships play their role but the humanistic side of relationships is gradually loosing its significance.

It is very important to maintain human relations as one becomes more successful. It's difficult as one gets less time due to a busy schedule as one becomes more successful. Another aspect is – not everybody likes it if you become successful. There will be some jealous people as well as some opponents. One has to manage them. In managing such people, one has to be strict and professional. Relation maintenance is not important in such cases. Success need not be about human relations. It depends on your hard work and determination, but maintaining good human relations will help you in maintaining the success. Success is only a momentary gain but human relations last lifelong. Any person who is not successful will definitely lose out in the long run.

●●

# Censorship is the Need of the Hour

Variation leads to a situation where one loses trust. So if we hear something with variable meanings, we too will be in conflict about which is right and which is wrong.

The newspaper was developed to make people defeat the cruel British, by making people aware about cruelty. But today, as the newspapers are losing the trust of the people, one wonders how they will defeat issues like corruption. So the Government of India for the purpose of restoring trust, and not to influence the information contained in the news scrutinizes the content in newspaper.

Even with technology at its peak in the modern era worldwide, it is not possible to censor selectively a part of the programs being telecasted and leave the other. What needs to be done is to have a common vote between the younger generation and their parents about the possible benefits and also ill effects of foreign channels. On one hand, channels like Discovery, Animal Planet, Star Sports, etc., provide us with the knowledge and entertainment not imparted by an Indian channel, while on the other hand there are channels like Fashion TV (which can be knowledgeable for followers of fashion) which are quite bad for kids in their developing age. In case of TV, the major issue is setting the right age limit for viewing adult content, as otherwise children get exposed to such stuff at a much earlier age.

So, a common forum should be set up between youngsters and elders on what to watch and at what age. Also, some relaxations should be given to the children. There is a saying, "curiosity killed the cat". This thing should always be kept in mind. Children should be left free to exercise their judgement to a certain extent so as not to let them feel that they are being pulled down. What I wish to convey here is that stop the children in the best manner possible and do not pressurize them at any stage as that can lead to more damage.

Media can be a doubled edged sword if not handled properly. In my point of view censorship is needed for such programmes where vulgar stuff is shown and which corrupts the minds of young people. On the other hand important programmes should not be censored. The second point which I would like to mention over here is that telecasts showing cheap publicity stunts should be censored, e.g., the one of model Poonam Pandey.

●●

# Education and success - Is there a Correlation?

Do you think there is any correlation which exists between Education and Success?

Bill Gates who is one of world's richest man despite dropping out of college is a great example that there is supposedly very little or no correlation. Dhirubhai Ambani is also a famous example in this category that needs a mention. What a person learns and what he really wants to do have no correlation many a times. But the fact is that a person succeeds only if he likes what he does. But while one can achieve success without education, there is no doubt that education brings richness in one's life. There is also no two ways to the fact that one is able to appreciate many facets of life due to the extended knowledge that education provides.

Although the topic began with famous examples of individuals who have emerged successful without education, there is nothing wrong in aspiring to become successful and a highly educated person.

In the past there have been people who have touched the peak of success in spite of not being from well-educated backgrounds. However, we cannot ignore the fact that education is a key to success. Education helps us in every step. Good education helps us to achieve higher success by providing us with information and skills that will equip us to fight our battles in life.

For example, if you do not know how to read and write, you are bound to face trouble finding a job because almost every job requires some kind of paperwork to read or fill out. Knowledge in mathematics is important for figuring out your salary or bank details and so on so forth. The more you know, the more likely you will excel at your job instead of struggling to survive in a work environment.

Several rich and successful people don't have many degrees but they have good ideas. They are smart, and because they don't have degrees doesn't mean they don't have the knowledge. Bill Gates was smart enough to know that getting a higher degree or a degree would have cost him everything he has today, because the time to capitalize on the market was when he did, not another three years or so down the road.

To be successful one needs information or knowledge. If you want to start a software company it would require lots of technical knowledge. If you want to start a luxury restaurant you need to know about luxury cuisine. So at every step you will need education. Even to start a restaurant you need a hotel management degree along with knowledge of certain secret family recipes. You can be very successful at what you started but success will depend on your skills, knowledge and desire to succeed.

On the other hand it is not that any correlation is necessary between success and education. Hard work is a must for success in any field but this doesn't mean that education is not necessary. It definitely guides us in how we plan our life.

# We don't learn from history, we Repeat it

The answer is more complex than it seems. Maybe the right question is: Does one learn the right lessons from history? In general, in history good things and bad things have happened and one tries to repeat the good ones and not repeat the bad ones. So if it turns out that ignoring Hitler's rise was a catastrophic and expensive mistake then one tries to prevent it happening again. And if a reality show turn out to be a hit TV show then everyone follows the trend of reality shows.

Most people or at least the leading thinkers in a position of responsibility try to learn from history. But the problem with history is that it s a lot better at telling you what you should have done yesterday than what you should do tomorrow. So even though appeasing Hitler turned out to be a great mistake it isn't all that obvious that we should attack North Korea for threatening its neighbours, and selling missiles and weapons to sundry despots. Nor is it obvious that we should attack Iran because its leader is developing nuclear weapons and says he believes Israel should not exist – even though that is as close as we will probably get to an analogy with Hitler. So with Iran, one analysis goes that we have another Hitler in the making and another one goes that we just have a domestic political leader with failed economic policies, with rapidly falling domestic popularity and his allies losing elections. He is trying out the tried and true method of autocrats of distracting people from his own failings by creating an ominous external enemy who is even worse than him. Hitler did mostly the same thing too, but on the other hand Hitler had managed to grab absolute power and Ahmedinejad will probably just lose the next election. You may disagree with my analysis, but that is the whole point.

Different people will have a different analysis and though most analyses will seem reasonable in prospect only one will turn out to be correct in retrospect. Each person doing a very contradictory analysis will have some facts and events in history to support their analysis – which is why every analysis is reasonable. That is just it about history; it is great at saying why something happened yesterday and not so good at saying what will happen tomorrow.

And apart from this example, there are plenty of examples where it is debatable what we should learn from history. Does the Hitler or Rwanda experience tell us that we must intervene in Darfur? Or does the Somalia or South Africa (peaceful defeat of apartheid) experience tell us that we should not militarily intervene? History tells us the strengths and weaknesses of the choices we made – it does not really tells us the strengths and weaknesses of the choices we did not make. We do not know whether intervening in Rwanda would have prevented a massacre (like in Kosovo) or simply let the massacre happen anyway despite intervention (like in Somalia) and given us a black eye in the process.

A famous quote says, "Life is a lousy teacher, she gives you the test first and the lesson afterwards". That, unfortunately, is how history works.

Historians tell us that if we don't learn about history, we're bound to repeat it. So lately I've been delving into old research papers here at the Center for Rural Affairs, hoping past research will inform our current research on health care. What I've found so far is astounding.

# If there were no Armies in the World

Imagine there were no armies across the border of two long time rivals since 1947, i.e., India and Pakistan then both the countries could have spent much more money on their development instead of granting humongous amounts of money to the defense sector in the budget. Indian government has been spending billions of rupees each and every year on defense, so that the Indian people and Indian geographical borders could be safe from any intruders or countries with malicious intentions. So is the case with Pakistan. They do not have electricity even in their major cities like Rawalpindi, Islamabad, Lahore and so on. The latter's social, political and, economical situation has been deteriorating after the political maestro Zulfikar Ali Bhutto's reign. Same is the situation in India but still life is better here compared to there.

There will still be disputes between individuals, communities, races, religions, economic classes, and countries. But as long as every government provides a police force dedicated exclusively to protecting citizen rights, and a court of law remains to decide what is just case-by-case, humanity stands a chance at prosperity. The odds against our continued survival in the universe are already too enormous for us to continue to sabotage ourselves with war. Global cooperation is becoming necessary. It could be achieved without dictatorial control, if only all nations could come to an agreement on what our priorities are as a species. The first priority is to end military war on Earth. Competition through creation with a timed goal is ultimately more stimulating for businesses and countries than a war industry with no end in sight. Also it is deadly hypocrisy to create a life and then instruct that child that ending life is okay as long as it's overseas and pays for college. People in warring countries could protest more effectively by refusing to have children until there is peace, and those who have children should inform them that their best protest is to not participate in war.

But what can an individual do? If an individual is sitting silent and then being attacked then he/she would have to retaliate in order to retain his/her dignity and to save his/her well wishers as well.

If there were no armies, then we would not have to worry about our borders, there will not be any defense budget, there will be no missile testing and there will not be any fear of nuclear holocaust and catastrophic loss of which folks and the personnel on the higher administrative or political posts are afraid of.

The big question is about trust and, this is the thing which we cannot rely upon because of betrayal that many of us have already faced in our lives and, we just cannot trust other countries for the sake of our people's lives. And, this will always lead us to live in the fear of catastrophic loss which may force us to confront terrorist acts, retaliation, and attack on the country.

Some additional disadvantage of absence of armies are: hypocrisy imposed by certain groups, law on paper will be biased, violence as no one will be there to stop them and finally, these things will create the platform to build an army and in this case nothing could be done. We will have to live like this only to protect ourselves from others. So the subject was never obsolete and never will be.

●●

## Wisdom does not come with Age

Wisdom does not automatically come with age, though it does for a lot of people. But there are some pretty ignorant people too. Nothing comes with age alone except wrinkles. Wisdom comes only from experience.

Researchers in positive psychology have defined wisdom as the coordination of “knowledge and experience” and “its deliberate use to improve well-being”.

A wise person’s actions are consistent with his/her ethical beliefs.

Wisdom is a deep and wide understanding of the word that we live in. That understanding relates to people, situations, events, habits, rules and things. This understanding helps us to act in a best way in specific situation. Wisdom does not necessarily depend on intellect and education, but is more related to experience, flexibility, willingness to understand others, ability to change and adopt. It is said that wisdom comes with the age.Although grandmothers tend to have an answer for everything, scientists warn us, based on extensive research, that wisdom does not come always with age. The researchers concluded that older people are not necessarily wiser than younger ones and that in some situations, react unreasonably.

Studies have shown that the wise constitute less than 1% of the population. This becomes visible in situations when it is necessary to solve problems, since people usually get too emotional. “It is easier to give wise counsel to others than ourselves.” This applies especially to older people The study showed that older people had worse results than the young in the evaluation of their virtues and weaknesses. Staudinger argues that this is because in the last phase of life people think about their whole life and they try to distinguish the positive events that would keep them from the bitterness of bad things. In addition, older people are less critical of themselves, while younger people more easily analyze their life.

Wisdom does not come necessarily with age. The ability of being wise is not directly related to aging, but to what we experience and how we perceive, memorize and use this experience in the future. Ability to accept changes is very important for making wise decisions. We are living in the age of rapid changes. What was fact yesterday could be obsolete today. Accepting the new things and using the experience from the past can help you in making good decisions.

Do not expect to become wise just because today you are older than yesterday. Do not expect to be appreciated by others, only based on your age. Be wiser by accepting new things and knowledge. Be ready to admit mistakes. Do not reject the opinion of others. Wisdom is the ability that can be learned and improved. It takes time and requires openness, but the result justifies the effort. Be wiser today than you were yesterday.

# Management education – is it necessary to Succeed in business?

In the present day world of business, where management rules each aspect of our life, it is very essential for an individual to understand the essence of management at least to the relative terms. This is because; the world has become so complex with the times that it would not function at all when "management" is not there.

When we take up the topic of business, we can look into the past where business was carried out since primitive ages. Only the size, nature, and complexity have changed. Doing business, possessing the qualities of a businessman is an inborn or inner trait of an individual. It was present even in our ancestors who had laid down the bases of business earlier, though at a small scale.

But the scenario has changed with the fast paced world. With industrialization bringing the entire world under one network, the need for "managing" such a huge complex and multidimensional world is felt which can't be done without proper guidance and training. Having understood the need of the upcoming markets and its trend, "management education" has spread all over the world and is helping the aspirant entrepreneurs or the professionals to get the latest knowledge and skills as per the need and expectations of the developments in business. The Education system in India is limited to theoretical knowledge that is confined to just some degrees. But "management education" gives practical knowledge importance over theoretical approach. This gives a complete understanding of the activities of business and the role required to be played by the individuals at a later stage. It's not that businesses cannot run without management education. But now, with the increasing competitiveness all over the world, to become a cut over the edge, the upcoming generations of professionals need to possess the required qualities of making their place in the tough competition by constant innovation and logical and analytical thinking. And "management education" adds these to an individual's personality.

Business is required to be managed, and Management is the backbone of business. Hence, both "management" and "business" go hand in hand and that contributes to the growth of the business at a worldwide scale.

The founder of Dell, Michael Dell did not have any management education. In fact, Michael Dell did not excel academically but had great business instincts. Mukesh Ambani did not have any management education either. He went to college and graduated with a Bachelor's degree in chemical engineering. He did later pursue his MBA from Stanford but did not complete the course.

Education is also not the key to success, great ideas are. Anyone can have education and a degree, but having great ideas is what separates people from the rest of the pack. A person's education does not translate into whether they have good or bad ideas either.

Bill Gates dropped out of college, technology was being released and Bill saw it as a great business opportunity. Luckily he had great support in his parents and a great idea. So Bill Gates, the richest man in the world is another person without any sort of management education.

On the other hand, we've had thousands if not millions of people who have had management education over the years yet most of those businesses have failed. It's all about having a great idea and the intelligence to know what the next big great idea is and plan for it.

●●

# The changing role of Women in India

Women's roles in India have been changing and women are now emerging from the past traditions into a new era of freedom and rights. Women now play as important a role as any man in the development of any nation, more so the Indian nation. Women have made their presence felt in every field. And they are second to none. A country like India has a lady as the President of the country. Even a superpower like USA is likely to have a woman President in the next elections. One must not underestimate or question women power.

In the past, women have been oppressed to a point where they were treated as a completely different species. They were in a country that seemed to be a dark tunnel with no hope, dreams, or sense of fulfillment. Now women have been given their natural birthrights, and they are able to do everything that males can.

Women in India are beginning to follow the direction that the women of the Western world took more than 80 years ago; demanding treatment as human equals. However, it has become more and more evident as the revolution ages that Indian women may have to adapt the Western feminist method to their very traditional and religious culture. India has different complications that put the development of women in a completely altered context than their Western counterparts. Although the key targets remain similar: improvement of health care, education and job opportunities in order to gain equality between men and women in the various settings of public society, the workplace, the school yard and – possibly the most fundamental setting of all – the home. Women are striving to be independent and be on an equal footing with men. The additional complexities that the women of India must also challenge are the caste system, the heavy religious customs, older and more traditional roles of the sexes, as well as the even stronger power that men hold in India. The status was at one time accepted, but with the Western women's revolution and perception, the role is slowly succeeding in its development through both independent groups of women, and national and worldwide organizations based on the goal of gaining equality. They have all accomplished much, but have yet to overthrow the male dominated society.

We are living in a democratic country and we are definitely open to outside influences. Media keeps us informed about changes occurring elsewhere, particularly in the western society where women are gaining an increasing respect. Here also the mentality is fast changing. The concept of equality is gaining ground and women are no longer regarded as inferior.

The Indian society is now proud of outstanding women achievers like Kalpana Chawla, Sania Mirza, Barkha Dutt, Shabana Azmi and many more. In a society where it was once unheard of for women to even be educated, women take up the majority of grade school teachers, and many more have blossomed into college professors with Ph D's and MD's. As women kept making these advancements to individualism, people have taken notice, and now women are considered better contenders for many jobs, men no longer have the full control they once fabricated. With the achievement of all this, women now have so many opportunities that were once a dream, the tunnel they once envisioned so dark and impassible seems like a stairway to light, to the open society of acceptance and opportunity. The future of women in India looks brighter and secured and their role even more important than just being a wife, mother, or daughter.

●●

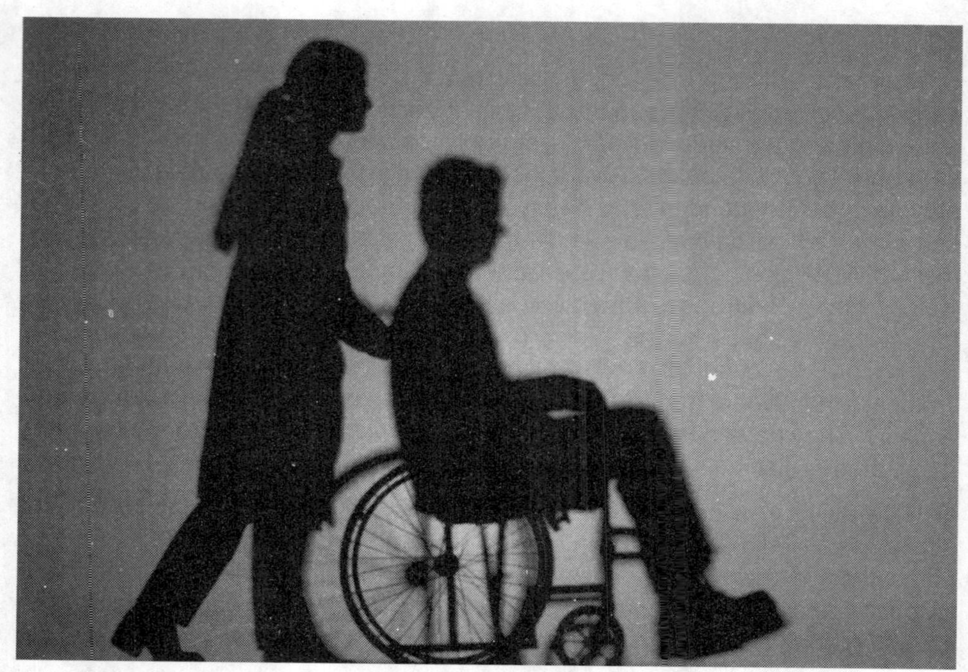

# NGOs...role in bringing Development

After the Second World War, welfare issues globally were the responsibility of the State. It is said that the adoption of the welfare principle was to make services available and accessible to the whole population in such ways as would not involve users in any humiliating loss of status, dignity or self-respect. This also includes the direct provision of the services and "agenda setting" which is defined as bringing welfare issues to the attention of the relevant decision makers. The oil price rise of 1973 triggered the first world-wide recession which brought the return of mass unemployment throughout the west, eroding what had been for the founders of the welfare state one of its supporting "pillars". This made it difficult and impossible for governments to continue with universal welfare issues.

The task of development became overwhelmingly challenging on the part of governments. Citizens grew poor and poorer especially in the Third World Countries with alarming scarcity of goods and lack of sufficient provision of services. This led to the rise of NGOs to become partners in the development work and at the same time NGOs are being accused of trying to "crowd out" government process. The inability of governments to deliver sufficiently the promised goods and services eroded their legitimacy.

Governments themselves began to doubt their own development strategies and thus realized the need for radical change involving private organizations voluntarily formed by the people themselves. NGOs therefore increasingly have to take on all development work and at the same time NGOs are being accused of trying to "crowd out" the government.

Development is a progress of positive change quantitatively and qualitatively. Many people define it in their own context according to their surroundings and immediate needs. Some therefore define it as a process by which members of a society inspire themselves and their institutions in ways that enhance their ability to mobilize and manage resources sustainably to produce sustainable change and justify distributed improvements in their quality of life, consistent with their aims and aspirations. It is a process involving community participation in critically identifying and analyzing their needs and problems, setting goals and making their own decisions on sustainable use of available resources to improve their quality of life. This implies that it is a struggle against oppression and all that makes life less human. It is a process of building new communities and alternative structures, which empower the poor and enable all people to become subjects of their own destiny. It involves a movement from unequal relationships to the democratization of all aspects of life and true self-reliance. In essence, development is about people and the way they live and every society/community must initiate its own development process and the government should mainly facilitate the process through good/democratic policies.

Another reason for the existence of NGOs is that people come together in independent groups to promote some type of activity that is not being undertaken by governments. Alternatively, governments may already be involved in an activity but groups are formed in order to challenge the way government is handling it.

Formation of NGOs require innovative thinking, creativity, conceptualization of vision, ability to assess an existing gap in the provision of a service(s) or goods which calls for the skills to analyze what is and what ought to be – the real and the ideal.

Most founders of successful NGOs have abilities of interpreting the past (history), assess the present and forecast the future relatively accurately and realistically. They have an ability to influence and mobilize popular support from beneficiaries, government and other possible state holders. They are good at planning, have entrepreneurial and managerial skills, are willing to work voluntarily, at least in the formative stages, should be able to understand the culture and traditions of the target groups and be ready to move with and adapt to the changing environment. They should be clear on their geographical area of operation and have clearly stated missions and objectives.

# IPL

The Indian Premier League (IPL) is a professional league for Twenty20 cricket competition in India. It was initiated by the Board of Control for Cricket in India (BCCI), headquartered in Mumbai, and is supervised by BCCI Vice President Rajeev Shukla, who serves as the league's Chairman and Commissioner. It is currently contested by 10 teams consisting of players from around the world. It was started after an altercation between the BCCI and the Indian Cricket League.

In 2010, IPL became the first sporting event ever to be broadcast live on YouTube in association with Indiatimes. Its brand value is estimated to be around $3.67 billion in fourth season. According to the Annual Review of Global Sports Salaries by sportingintelligence.com, IPL is the second highest-paid league, based on first-team salaries on a pro rata basis, second only to the NBA. It is estimated that the average salary of an IPL player over a year would be $3.84 million.

## First season

The inaugural season of the tournament started on 18 April 2008 and lasted for 46 days with 59 matches scheduled, out of which 58 took place and 1 was washed out due to rain. The final was played in DY Patil Stadium, Nerul, Navi Mumbai. Every team played each other both at home and away in a round robin system. The top four ranking sides progressed to the knockout stage of semi-finals followed by a final. Rajasthan Royals defeated Chennai Super Kings in a last ball thriller and emerged as the inaugural IPL champions.

## Second season

The 2009 season coincided with the General Elections in India. Owing to concerns regarding players' security, the venue was shifted to South Africa. The format of the tournament remained same as the inaugural one. Deccan Chargers, who finished last in the first season were big underdogs, but came out as eventual winners defeating the Royal Challengers Bangalore in the final. Deccan set a target of 144 with the help of Gibbs(53) and defended it.

## Third season

The third season opened in January 2010 with the auction for players. 66 players were on offer but only 11 players were sold. In this season, Deccan Chargers did not play at their preferred home location of Hyderabad, India due to the ongoing political crisis in the Telangana region. The new bases for the champions this season were Nagpur, Navi Mumbai and Cuttack. Four teams qualified for the semi-finals. Mumbai Indians who defeated Bangalore Royal Challengers by 35 runs won the first semi-final. Chennai Super Kings defeated Deccan Chargers in the second semi-final. The final was played between Chennai Super Kings and Mumbai Indians. Chennai Super Kings won by a margin of 22 runs.

## Fourth season

On 21 March 2010, it was announced in Chennai that two new teams from Pune and Kochi will be added to the IPL for the fourth season. However, the bid around the Kochi franchisee turned controversial resulting in the resignation of minister, Shashi Tharoor from the Central Government and investigations by various departments of the Government of India into the financial dealings of IPL and the other existing franchisees. Later, Lalit Modi was also removed from IPL chairmanship by BCCI. On 5 December 2010, it was confirmed that Kochi will take part in the fourth season of IPL.

The addition of teams representing Pune and Kochi was to have increased the number of franchises from 8 to 10. The BCCI originally considered extending the tournament format used in previous season to ten teams, which would increase the number of matches from 60 to 94. Instead, the round-robin stage of the tournament was to have been replaced by a group stage with two groups of five, limiting the number of matches to 74. But this format was replaced by another one in which each team would play 5 other teams in a two-way round robin format and there would be 2 teams against whom they would play only at home and remaining 2 teams against which they would play only away matches. Thus each team plays 14 matches. Top four teams would qualify for the semifinals.

In October 2010, the Rajasthan Royals and Kings XI Punjab had their franchises terminated for breaching ownership rules. The new Kochi franchise was also issued a warning to resolve all their ownership disputes. Two months later both teams were finally allowed to take part in the 2011 edition after a court ruling.

Chennai Super Kings won their second consecutive IPL title after defeating Royal Challengers Bangalore by 58 runs in the fourth season of IPL. CSK had beaten RCB in the playoffs too while RCB defeated Mumbai Indians to reach the final. This is the first time a franchise has won two IPL titles, had four consecutive semi-final visits, come to the finals three times, and successfully defended their title. The top four teams namely CSK, RCB, KKR and MI have also qualified for the Champions League. Mumbai Indians are the current Champions League Twenty20 champions.

# Semester system education... Boon or Curse?

The semester system has its own merits, but it could have been designed better to accommodate non-academic activities and enhance deeper learning. According to teachers, one of the main advantages of the semester system is that it reduces students' burden. An academic year is divided into two terms called semesters. For example, if there are 10 subjects to study in a year, then it's equally divided for the semester. According to students, though this has helped them to prepare better for their exams, in-depth knowledge of subjects is missing.

In the semester system, there is no connection between semesters unlike in an annual system. In the annual system, there is complete knowledge about the subject. But, in the semester system, students tend to read what appears only for the exam. Hence, deeper knowledge about the subject is missing. Semester system is good if the question paper is more application-oriented, demanding each student to learn more about the subject," he added. The shift from annual to semester system is not easy. "In the semester system, you get only four months to complete the syllabus. Due to paucity of time, teachers will not be unable to complete the syllabus and students will be forced to leave out some chapters. But, if the semester system is designed well, it can lead to some first hand experience in the industry."

Semester system can prove to be very good if classes are held as per schedule. According to the University Grants Commission (UGC), it's 16-18 weeks in a semester but we get only 14-16 weeks. UGC also recommends 50-52 hours of course work but we do not get so much time. However, from the students' perspective, it is good as they will be able to concentrate better on the subject and perform well." Semester system gives less time for extra-curricular activities but it's fine as the focus is more on the course.

One school of thought feels that it's more of a burden on teachers as they may not be able to complete the syllabus and there is less scope for extra-curricular activities. Some syllabuses are designed in such a way that the workload for teachers was 60 hours per semester. But the duration of the semester was reduced to 90 working days — three months. So, a teacher is left with 48 hours to complete 60 hours of workload. This way they won't be able to do justice to the subject. Many teachers have expressed their unhappiness with the way the syllabus is covered, but they are helpless.

It's important to go out of the syllabus to create interest among students. The main objective of the semester system is to introduce different papers and different topics to increase students' knowledge. We need to prepare students for the job market but the syllabus coverage is purely exam-oriented. This system has hampered the meaning of true education.

Another school of thought are of the opinion that both the students and teachers find the semester system easy as they don't have to prepare the entire year for the exam. However, in the annual system, students have the tendency to take it easy.In a semester system there should be constant feedback from students so that teachers can take corrective measures. One cannot have a new system in the old structure. There can be multiple-choice questions for the semester system. It needs a different question paper pattern so that paper evaluation is quicker and teachers get extra time. The course should be made more practical. If not, it will end up becoming more system-oriented than student-oriented.

The semester system has many advantages. For instance, in an annual system, you will have to study 10-12 subjects at once. But, in the semester system, subjects are divided equally. In the semester system, students have to be on their toes. They have to be focused. They cannot relax here. Initially, there were complaints that the semester system affected extra-curricular activities, but now, colleges have learnt to deal with this issue."

# Superstitions

Superstition is a belief in supernatural causality: that one event leads to the cause of another without any process in the physical world linking the two events. Opposition to superstition was a central concern of the intellectuals during the 18th century Age of Enlightenment. The philosophies at that time ridiculed any belief in miracles, revelation, magic, or the supernatural, as "superstition," and typically included as well much of Christian doctrine.

The word is often used pejoratively to refer to practices (e.g., Voodoo) other than the one prevailing in a given society (e.g., Christianity in western culture), although the prevailing religion may contain just as many supernatural beliefs. It is also commonly applied to beliefs and practices surrounding luck, prophecy and spiritual beings, particularly the belief that future events can be foretold by specific unrelated prior events.

Some common superstitions are as follows:

- A sack full of rice will be spoilt when touched by women in periods! It will also get spoilt if touched by women after having sex.
- Coconut Tree, Ashoka Tree, Banyan Tree, etc are considered sacred.
- The tail end of cows is considered as most sacred part as fortune Lakshmi lives there!
- The "VAASTU" as a guide for floor plans of a house is a superstitious system.
- East is the most preferred direction for all activities (I've seen some of them preferring to sit facing east even in the office).

- Do not proceed, if a cat crosses your way, it brings omen.
- Looking at cat in the morning is jinx.
- Looking at mother's face or picture of God as soon as you open your eyes in the morning will bring good luck for that day.
- Giving or taking anything in the left hand is bad (you know what left hand is used for in India).
- Never ask the question "where are you going?" while they are leaving house, its purpose will not be fulfilled.

People have superstitions because they allow fear and illogical thoughts to control their minds instead of thinking things through rationally.

One of the biggest superstitions in history is the Big Bang Theory. Evidence that scientists use to support this theory is incomplete and largely speculative. If the earth was formed as a result of a massive explosion billions of years ago, then how do you explain how the 'bang' material got there? Was it always there? Or who put it there? The answer: nobody. Some think The Big Bang is a lie. Human minds may never understand or comprehend the origins of life or the universe. Let's just say God created everything in existence. Of course, this second paragraph – which is more of an assumption – relies on an antiquated knowledge of matter and energy. Humans use the language they have at their disposal. In time, we'll have better terms to use to explain what is now called "Big Bang." Our limited perception of 'time' limits our ability to fully analyze that "point in time" The first paragraph actually is the best.

●●

# THE PUNISHMENT FOR BIGAMY: TWO MOTHERS-IN-LAW

## Bigamy

In cultures that practice marital monogamy, bigamy is the act of entering into a marriage with one person while still legally married to another. Bigamy is a crime in most western countries, and when it occurs in this context often neither the first nor second spouse is aware of the other. In countries that have bigamy laws, consent from a prior spouse makes no difference to the legality of the second marriage, which is usually considered void. Most western countries do not recognize polygamous marriages, and consider bigamy a crime. Several countries also prohibit people from living a polygamous lifestyle.

Bigamy is where a person gets a marriage license and marries another. Then, gets another marriage license and does it again. Sister wives has only one marriage license, the others are "committed" in a simple ceremony without a license, so the others apparently are not married as far as the state is concerned. The others may fall under "common law" however, where if you live together and act as a married couple, you eventually become a married couple under the law. The purpose is for things like inheritance of property. Common law marriages usually require a period of time. If common law applies to one or more of the women, then yes, he could be charged with bigamy, but not until the required time period has passed. Prosecution for bigamy is extremely rare and Mormons for example who practice this multiple wives thing are so careful to avoid conflicts with the law exactly in a case like this. I hardly think he would allow himself to be tripped up in so trivial manner. He seems smarter than that, at least from what I saw on the earlier programs. In the case of inheritance under common law, the non-owner can claim inheritance exactly like the surviving spouse in a marriage with a license can do. I don't think they were being serious.

Marriage ceremonies to more than one woman aren't required for you to be charged, just living together as a family can be sufficient.

Bigamy is the practice of being married to two people at once. This form of polygamy is considered illegal in many Western countries, and it has historically been a topic of contention, especially in the United States, where some Mormon sects support the practice of polygamy, and resent state interference in what they view as their private affairs. As a general rule, bigamy is rarely prosecuted, and when it is, the penalty varies; the primary spouse may be ordered to serve time in jail, and potentially to pay a fine, for example.

In a classic example of bigamy, a man marries a woman, and then marries another several years later, while he is still legally married to the first women. Depending on the culture in which the bigamy occurs, the second marriage may be undertaken with the full consent of both wives, or the second marriage may be concealed. Should the man take a third wife, he would be committing trigamy; if he added additional spouses to the mix, it would become polygamy, or, more accurately, polygyny.

Sometimes, people commit bigamy by accident, and there is some leeway in the law to provide for this. For example, if a couple separates but does not formally divorce and one spouse remarry, this could be considered a form of bigamy, but it is often permitted if the separation was more than five years ago, and the remarrying partner made a good faith effort to formally divorce the other. In some regions, if someone has been absent from a marriage for five or more years, he or she will be legally declared dead, allowing the surviving spouse to remarry without fear of bigamy charges.

In some regions of the world, bigamy is perfectly acceptable and commonplace, due to cultural or religious values. Some people feel that such marriages can be beneficial for those involved, allowing the partners to share the work in the marriage and can work together as a team. Others feel that bigamy exploits one or more of the people involved in the marriage, especially when a second wife is treated more like a household slave than a member of the family.

# Kids today are not what they Used to Be

James R. Flynn, an emeritus professor of political science at the University of Otaga in New Zealand, discovered two decades ago that IQ test scores were steadily rising in the developed world despite failing schools and stagnant standardized test scores – a phenomenon called the "Flynn effect". During a recent visit to UCLA, Flynn talked about the conundrum, which is the subject of his new book, "*What Is Intelligence?*"

Are children today smarter than their parents?

He was of the opinion that they think better on their feet; they can solve problems on the spot without being told what to do; they are better at working with shapes, thanks in part to the Internet and the computer.

If one asked a person in 1900 what a dog and rabbit had in common, they would say you could use a dog to hunt rabbits. Today you would say they both are mammals. That is shorthand for a lot of insight. That may seem trivial, but classifying the world is prerequisite to understanding it scientifically.

The environment in which kids grow up today are different. They are today exposed to different sources of media like radio, television, Internet, etc. They learn many things quicker and also mature faster. They can access a lot of information compared to earlier times. There are a lot of negative influences too. Kids are more demanding.

Today both parents go to work so they do not spend much time with their children and nor do they have time for holidays. This leads to a not very healthy lifestyle where they spend much time watching TV, especially those who are above 14 years. Watching inappropriate programs and not eating meals on time have become the norm. Finally they grow up to be spoilt individuals who care about no one but themselves.

From the education point of view, competition has become so fierce that it forces them to compete from the beginning. This leads to non-inculcation of values like sharing and giving.

In many respects today's kids are smarter, like when it comes to computers and gadgets. Mathematics it seems is becoming more prominent since a lot of programming and even some basic skills such as typing require a basic mathematical thought.

On the other hand, though kids are losing a lot of people skills. There are many kids in recent years, who are actually good at conversing, they seem to have gotten so used to texting and talking over e-mails and IM that they have lost some of their social skills of a face-to-face conversation or even writing a letter.

# Examinations – has it Killed Education?

The word education means "to bring out what is already in". Examination in our country has destroyed the true meaning of education. Instead today, students are more interested in getting good grades rather than acquiring true knowledge of the subject. Einstein said "Imagination is more important than knowledge" however examination has killed education and best example is the latest survey done by corporate India where it has declared that only 20% of the total graduates produced are talented or 20% have understood what has been taught to them.

Another example can be of the movie *3 Idiots* where only the lead actor Rancho, proved to be a true student because of his love for engineering, whereas rest of his friends found themselves struggling. Gaining good grades should not be the main motive of students instead they should excel in the field of their interest. Examination should be replaced by open book tests and group dynamics. Every student should be given opportunities in every field so that they recognize their potential better

Examinations cannot kill education. There must be some way for a person to know his/her level of understanding. Examination is a way to measure it. The way examinations are conducted has an impact on education. Examination must truly measure a person's understanding of the concept and must tests his/her application level of a certain concept. Instead examination encourages people to do rote learning.

Question papers do not have questions, which make students think. That's why only 1per cent students out of scores of students who take IIT-JEE or CAT, qualify for it. The methodology for conducting the exams must change which will change the way students learn. This will immensely help students as well as the society in producing real learners.

While it might be true that examinations as the sole criterion for judging performance might not be a good idea, examinations can still be used as one of the many performance criteria. Examinations can be combined with other tools like projects, assignments and presentations to judge a student's performance. The weightage for the different tools would have to be carefully chosen after taking into consideration the nature of the course as well as the depth of the course. If the subject calls for a mere understanding of the facts, the weightage of examinations can be more. However if the subject has more practical implementations, the weightage for the projects can be made substantially higher. Also rather than questioning the usefulness of exams, it would be better if we focus on the nature/quality of the questions in the examination. If the questions call for a mere cramming of the subject, it would not necessarily be a good judgement of the students' abilities. On the other hand, if the questions were to test the understanding of the concepts and the applications that it could have, it calls for a larger amount of analysis/thinking from the student. Such an examination would be more ideal to nudge the student.

Examination has not killed education; it is the method of examination which is responsible for it. The reason for this is because it's more theoretical than practical. This is why many of the students need to mug up. They need to remember lots of explanation with points. If it will be more objective then students will learn it practically and also will start implementing the things, which they have learnt in day-to-day life.

Examination leads to competition among students so students should understand the importance of education and examination. Education is for gaining knowledge and examinations are to know where we are standing in this competitive world and how much more concentration or attention they need to pay to survive.

# Are beauty pageants Necessary?

A beauty "pageant" or beauty contest is a competition that focuses on the physical beauty of its contestants, although such contests often incorporate personality, talent, and answers to judges' questions as judged criteria. The phrase almost invariably refers only to contests for women; similar events for men are called by other names and are more likely to be "body building" contests. Winners of beauty contests are often called beauty queens.

Each year, cohorts of women sashay across stages flashing brilliant white smiles. They parade in swimsuits in front of vast audiences, all in the hope of being named the fairest of all present. Beauty pageants are a norm in today's society, receiving both recognition and acclaim for their efforts in locating and honouring pretty faces. The winner gets her radiant face plastered across papers the next day and eventually triumphs to become a movie star. Despite such social acceptance, beauty pageants have been criticized as a senseless waste of time and resources.

How exactly would one define beauty?

Like all adjectives, its definition actually depends on comparisons. Any girl would be stunning next to a hippopotamus but not necessarily so when compared to other females. Is it possible to enact a law stating that "beauty" should consist of translucent skin, large eyes and high cheekbones? The so-called fairest of them all is merely fair by the judges' ideas of beauty. Is choosing the supposedly most attractive woman as important as a cure for cancer? The winner is draped with a sash, receives a bouquet of flowers, gets her picture in the news and then? And then nothing! Man does not profit from it. The dying still die, the starving still starve and the winner will be reduced to ashes once her successor ascends the throne.

The worst is yet to come. The organizers realized just how purposeless lining up these girls and evaluating their faces was. So, they attempted more. They started firing questions at the contestants for evidence that beauty and brains can co-exist. What a flop! The questions released a storm of broken English and a distressing lack of general knowledge. So what if the winners contribute to the film industry? Beauty pageants are incapable of producing truly beautiful women, in the fullest sense of the term "beautiful". The fact that they are still in existence is nothing short of a miracle only outdone by the millions who still want to participate in them.

The question is, "Is the holding of yearly beauty contests a necessary thing to do?" What is beauty? Is it the mind, from the heart or the face? There are so many women physically disfigured through some sort of illness or naturally born with deformity or handicap, who may feel somehow psychologically depressed or rejected in the society when they watch beauty contests.

Scientists have come out with great inventions but no one has been able to replace God's creation of a human being and pushed breath in him yet. So how can a panel of judges declare one as beautiful and the other ugly? Howsoever a woman looks, society must accept and give her the respect she deserves.

In a way beauty contests are meaningless. The late Princess Diana was one of the most beautiful women in the world, but newspapers reported her as a woman who suffered in silence leading to her untimely death. If beauty had played an all-important role in her life, and had given her all the happiness she was looking for from her husband, Prince Charles, she might well be alive today.

●●

# Terrorism

The word "terrorism" is politically and emotionally charged, and this greatly compounds the difficulty of providing a precise definition. Studies have found over 100 definitions of "terrorism". The concept of terrorism may itself be controversial as it is often used by state authorities to delegitimize political or other opponents, and potentially legitimize the state's own use of armed force against opponents (such use of force may itself be described as "terror" by opponents of the state).

Terrorism has been practiced by a broad array of political organizations for furthering their objectives. It has been practiced by right-wing and left-wing political parties, nationalistic groups, religious groups, revolutionaries, and ruling governments. An abiding characteristic is the indiscriminate use of violence against noncombatants for the purpose of gaining publicity for a group, cause, or individual.

Terrorist attacks are usually carried out in such a way as to maximize the severity and length of the psychological impact. Each act of terrorism is a "performance" devised to have an impact on many large audiences. Terrorists also attack national symbols, to show power and to attempt to shake the foundation of the country or society they are opposed to. This may negatively affect a government, while increasing the prestige of the given terrorist organization and/or ideology behind a terrorist act.

Terrorist acts frequently have a political purpose. Terrorism is a political tactic, like letter writing or protesting, which is used by activists when they believe that no other means will affect the kind of change they desire. Change is desired so badly that failure to achieve change is seen as a worse outcome than the deaths of civilians. This is often where the inter-relationship between terrorism and religion occurs.

Very often, the victims of terrorism are targeted not because they are threats, but because they are specific "symbols, tools, animals or corrupt beings" that tie into a specific view of the world that the terrorists possess. Their suffering accomplishes the terrorists' goals of instilling fear, getting their message out to an audience or otherwise satisfying the demands of their often radical religious and political agendas.

The recent attacks in Mumbai have had negative impact on the financial capital of India, making it clear that there is something lacking in our defense security to protect the population of the country.

The Indian government has to take drastic action on its territory. The reality is, there is great dissatisfaction within society, which is causing these failures in security, the lack of sympathy and support from the government, with its population regardless of religion or philosophy that will continue. The development of India depends, on the anti-terrorist policy, which this government applies. The economic situation is directly connected to these conditions, and the poverty and the non-existent welfare will be a serious danger.

●●

# Impact of television Reality Shows on Children

Reality shows have gained increasing and enormous popularity in India. Be it a reality show like "*Big Boss*", or an adventurous reality television show like "*Is Jungle Se Mujhe Bachao*", the one common factor between every reality show is the fact that it affects and influences children. Influence can be both positive and negative.

In a reality show like "*Is Jungle Se Mujhe Bachao*", there was adventure and excitement on nearly every aspect of the show because it was in a jungle setting, with the celebrity contestants living amongst the wilderness and the wild. This brought an edge to the show because of the varied and sometimes, creepy adventures the contestants experience in the show. Children seeing this do not necessarily read the disclaimer or notice that comes before the show. Also, in India we do not have a concept of rating TV shows as PG-13 or A or U. This makes it incredibly sensitive for kids to view this show. If they do, what is the guarantee that they are not going to try stunts at home? What is the guarantee that they are not going to start to bottle up live cockroaches? This is why the TV shows have to be viewed with discretion and if children watch a show like this, then they have to be properly explained as to how these stunts simply cannot be tried out anywhere by them, and this explanation might have to be repeated several times by an adult.

Kids today have reached another level of smartness. This allows them to realize that reality shows have many aspects that are real in nature. They understand and differentiate between reality and non-reality based TV programs. Kids do not always see reason and this is why there is a negative influence of TV on them.

A reality show like "*Big Boss*" was seen to be exceeding TRP ratings, is watched by children as well as adults with equal enthusiasm. There is intrigue in watching people lead their 90 days of their life in the vicinity of an enclosure, which brings to light emotions and drama and one would wonder whether this has a positive, negative or any influence at all on children. And voila, it does! It has sometimes, a neutral effect on children because often, there is no significant impact that is had on children by viewing a normal TV show like "*Big Boss*" but the fact that they portray drama and emotions, running wild at times, gives ideas to children and this leans towards negative influence.

Positive shows are shows that send out good, strong messages to the youth. Even shows like *Sa-Re-Ga-Ma-Pa, Dance India Dance, Boogie Woogie,* etc., which has children of different age groups singing, dancing and performing in the children segments of the show, create a fierce sense of competition in the participants and this is not healthy as children should understand that competition is meant to only be healthy otherwise it's not like a competition it's like a feud. Children who watch these shows get carried away and there is a possibility they may begin to ignore their education in the quest of the hope to reach the level a participant of his age or liking has in the competition. These are the various impacts that reality TV shows have on children.

"Children are like wet cement. Whatever falls on them makes an impression."

Don't be disheartened if you did not do well in your first Group Discussion. The best possible preparation for a Group Discussion is to learn from one's past mistakes.

Children should be encouraged to watch shows that are suitable for them and also the media should maintain ethical constrains in the programs they air, keeping in mind the viewership.

# Sex Education

Sex education refers to formal programs of instruction on a wide range of issues relating to human sexuality, including human sexual anatomy, sexual reproduction, sexual intercourse, reproductive health, emotional relations, reproductive rights and responsibilities, abstinence, contraception, and other aspects of human sexual behavior. Common avenues for sex education are parents or caregivers, school programs, and public health campaigns.

Human sexuality has biological, emotional/physical or spiritual aspects. The biological aspect of sexuality refers to the reproductive mechanism as well as the basic biological drive that exists in all species, which is hormonally controlled. The emotional or physical aspect of sexuality refers to the bond that exists between individuals, and is expressed through profound feelings or physical manifestations of emotions of love, trust, and caring. There is also a spiritual aspect of sexuality of an individual or as a connection with others. Experience has shown that adolescents are curious about some or all the aspects of their sexuality as well as the nature of sexuality in general and that many will wish to experience their sexuality.

Traditionally, adolescents were not given any information on sexual matters, with discussion of these issues being considered taboo. Such instruction as was given was traditionally left to a child's parents, and often this was put off until just before a child's marriage. Most of the information on sexual matters were obtained informally from friends and the media, and much of this information was of doubtful value. Much of such information was usually known to be deficient, especially during the period following puberty when curiosity of sexual matters was the most acute. This deficiency became increasingly evident by the increasing incidence of teenage pregnancies, especially in Western countries after the 1960s. As part of each country's efforts to reduce such pregnancies, programs of sex education were instituted, initially over strong opposition from parents and religious groups.

Sexuality is an important aspect of the life of a human being and almost all the people including children want to know about it. Sex education stands for protection, presentation extension, improvement and development of the family based on accepted ethical ideas. Thus, sex education may also be described as "sexuality education", which means that it encompasses education about all aspects of sexuality, including information about family planning, reproduction (fertilization, conception and development of the embryo and fetus, through to childbirth), plus information about all aspects of one's sexuality including body image, sexual orientation, sexual pleasure, values, decision-making, communication, dating, relationships, sexually transmitted infections (STIs) and how to avoid them, and birth control methods. Various aspect of sex education are to right school depending on the age of the students or what the children are able to comprehend at a particular point in time. Many experts have expressed that sex education is not merely a unit in reproduction and teaching how babies are conceived and born. It has a far richer scope and goal of helping the youngster incorporate sex most meaningfully into his present and future life, to provide him with some basic understanding on virtually every aspect of sex by the time he reaches full maturity.

Sex education may be taught informally, such as when someone receives information from a conversation with a parent, friend, religious leader, or through the media. It may also be delivered through sex self-help authors, magazine advice columnists, sex columnists, or sex education web sites. Formal sex education occurs when schools or health care providers offer sex education. Slyer stated that sex education teaches the young person what he or she should know for his or her personal conduct and relationship with others.

Sometimes formal sex education is taught as a full course as part of the curriculum in junior high school or high school. Other times it is only one unit within a more broad biology class, health class, home economics class, or physical education class. Some schools offer no sex education, since it remains a controversial issue in several countries, particularly the United States (especially with regard to the age at which children should start receiving such education, the amount of detail that is revealed, and topics dealing with human sexual behaviour, e.g. safe sex practices, masturbation, premarital, and sexual ethics).

Majority of people favours some sort of sex instruction in public schools, and this has become an intensely controversial issue because unlike most subjects, sex education is concerned with an especially sensitive and highly personal part of human life. He suggested that sex education should be taught in the classroom. The problem of pregnancy in adolescents is delicate and difficult to assess using sex education.

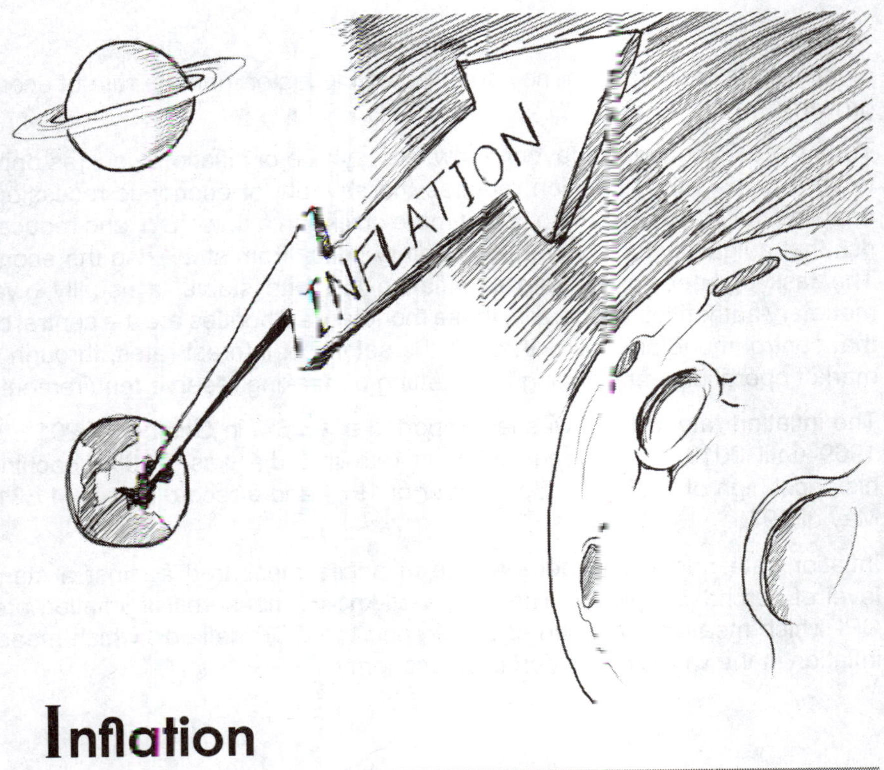


# Inflation

Inflation, in Economics, is a rise in the general level of prices of goods and services in an economy over a period of time. When the general price level rises, each unit of currency buys fewer goods and services. Consequently, inflation also reflects to anerosion in the purchasing power of money – a loss of real value in the internal medium of exchange and unit of account in the economy. A chief measure of price inflation is the inflation rate, the annualized percentage change in a general price index (normally the Consumer Price Index) over time.

Inflation's effects on an economy are various and can be simultaneously positive and negative. Negative effects of inflation include a decrease in the real value of money and other monetary items over time, uncertainty over future inflation may discourage investment and savings, and high inflation may lead to shortages of goods if consumers begin hoarding out of concern that prices will increase in the future. Positive effects include ensuring central banks can adjust nominal interest rates (intended to mitigate recessions), and encouraging investment in non-monetary capital projects.

Economists generally agree that high rates of inflation and hyperinflation are caused by an excessive growth of the money supply. Views on which factors determine low to moderate rates of inflation are more varied. Low or moderate inflation may be attributed to fluctuations in real demand for goods and services, or changes in available supplies such as during scarcities, as well as to growth in the money supply. However, the consensus view is that a long sustained period of inflation is caused by money supply growing faster than the rate of economic growth.

Today, most economists favour a low, steady rate of inflation. Low (as opposed to zero or negative) inflation reduces the severity of economic recessions by enabling the labour market to adjust more quickly in a downturn, and reduces the risk that a liquidity trap prevents monetary policy from stabilizing the economy. The task of keeping the rate of inflation low and stable is usually given to monetary authorities. Generally, these monetary authorities are the central banks that control monetary policy through the setting of interest rates, through open market operations, and through the setting of banking reserve requirements.

The inflation rate in India was last reported at 9.36% in October of 2011. From 1969 until 2010, the average inflation rate in India was 7.99% reaching an historical high of 34.68% in September of 1974 and a record low of –11.31% in May of 1976.

Inflation rate refers to a general rise in prices measured against a standard level of purchasing power. The most well-known measures of inflation are the CPI which measures consumer prices, and the GDP deflator, which measures inflation in the whole of the domestic economy.

# Surrogacy

Surrogacy is an arrangement in which a woman carries and delivers a child for another couple or person. This woman, the surrogate mother, may be the child's genetic mother (called traditional surrogacy), or she may be biologically unrelated to the child (called gestational surrogacy).

If the surrogate receives compensation beyond the reimbursement of medical and other reasonable expenses, the arrangement is called commercial surrogacy, otherwise it is often referred to as altruistic surrogacy.

In a traditional surrogacy the child may be conceived via home artificial insemination using fresh or frozen sperm or impregnated via IUI (intrauterine insemination), or ICI (intracervical insemination) performed at a health clinic. Because gestational surrogacy requires the implantation of a previously created embryo, that process always takes place in a clinical setting.

The intended parents, sometimes called the social parents, may arrange a surrogate pregnancy because of homosexuality, female infertility, or other medical issues which make pregnancy or delivery impossible, risky or otherwise undesirable. The intended parent may also be a single man or woman wishing to have his/her own biological child. Although the idea of vanity surrogacy is a common trope in popular culture and anti-surrogacy arguments, there is little or no data showing that women choose surrogacy for reasons of aesthetics or convenience.

Having another woman bear a child for a couple to raise, usually with the male half of the couple as the genetic father, is referred to in antiquity. Babylonian law and custom allowed this practice and infertile woman could use the practice to avoid the divorce which would otherwise be inevitable.

In the United States, the issue of surrogacy was widely publicized in the case of Baby M, in which the surrogate and biological mother of Melissa Stern ("Baby M"), born in 1986, refused to cede custody of Melissa to the couple with whom she had made the surrogacy agreement. The courts of New Jersey found that Mary Beth Whitehead was the child's legal mother and declared contracts for surrogate motherhood illegal and invalid. However, the court found it in the best interests of the infant to award custody of Melissa to her biological father William Stern and his wife Elizabeth Stern, rather than to the surrogate mother Mary Beth Whitehead.

There have been cases of clashes between surrogate mothers and the genetic parents; when unexpected complications with the fetus makes the genetic parents ask for an abortion even though the surrogate mother is opposing the abortion.

The historical legal assumption has been that the woman giving birth to a child is that child's legal mother, and the only way for another woman to be recognized as the mother is through adoption (usually requiring the birth mother's formal abandonment of parental rights).

Even in jurisdictions that do not recognize surrogacy arrangements, if the genetic parents and the birth mother proceed without any intervention from the government and have no changes of heart along they way, they will likely be able to achieve the effects of surrogacy by having the surrogate mother give birth and then give the child up for private adoption to the intended parents.

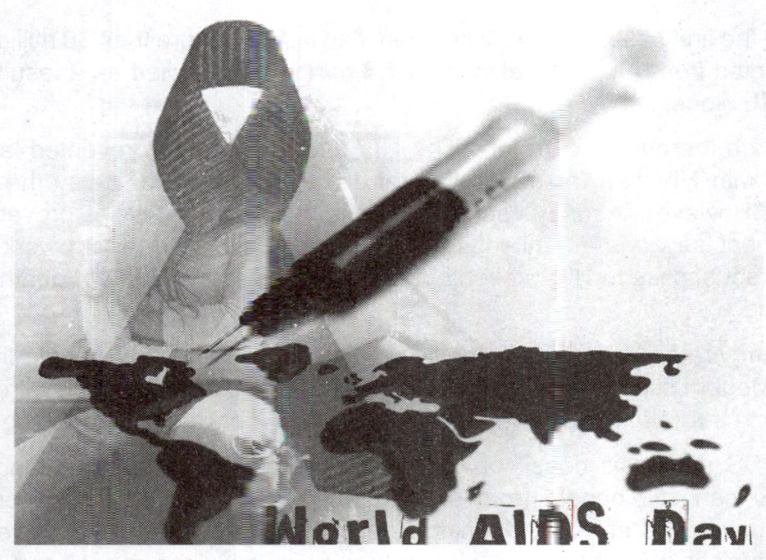


# AIDS

AIDS stands for: Acquired Immune Deficiency Syndrome. AIDS is a medical condition. A person is diagnosed with AIDS when their immune system is too weak to fight off infections. Since AIDS was first identified in the early 1980s, an unprecedented number of people have been affected by the global AIDS epidemic. Today, there are an estimated 34 million people living with HIV and AIDS worldwide.

AIDS is caused by HIV.

HIV is a virus that gradually attacks immune system cells. As HIV progressively damages these cells, the body becomes more vulnerable to infections, which it will have difficulty in fighting off. It is at the point of very advanced HIV infection that a person is said to have AIDS. If left untreated, it can take around ten years before HIV has damaged the immune system enough for AIDS to develop.A person is diagnosed with AIDS when they have developed an AIDS related condition or symptom, called an opportunistic infection, or an AIDS related cancer. The infections are called 'opportunistic' because they take advantage of the opportunity offered by a weakened immune system.

It is possible for someone to be diagnosed with AIDS even if they have not developed an opportunistic infection. AIDS can be diagnosed when the number of immune system cells (CD4 cells) in the blood of an HIV positive person drops below a certain level.

Since the first cases of AIDS were identified in 1981, more than 30 million people have died from AIDS. An estimated 1.8 million people died as a result of AIDS in 2010 alone.

Although there is no cure for AIDS, HIV infection can be prevented, and those living with HIV can take antiretroviral drugs to prevent or delay the onset of AIDS. However, in many countries across the world access to prevention and treatment services is limited. Global leaders have pledged to work towards universal access to HIV prevention and care, so that millions of deaths can be averted.

Antiretroviral treatment can significantly prolong the lives of people living with HIV. Modern combination therapy is highly effective and someone with HIV who is taking treatment could live for the rest of their life without developing AIDS.

An AIDS diagnosis does not necessarily equate to a death sentence. Many people can still benefit from starting antiretroviral therapy even once they have developed an AIDS defining illness. Better treatment and prevention for opportunistic infections have also helped to improve the quality and length of life for those diagnosed with AIDS. It is also important that treatment is provided for AIDS related pain, which is experienced by almost all people in the very advanced stages of HIV infection. Even though antiretroviral treatment can prevent the onset of AIDS in a person living with HIV, many people are still diagnosed with AIDS today. There are four main reasons for this:

Many people are never tested for HIV and only become aware they are infected with the virus once they have developed an AIDS related illness. These people are at a higher risk of mortality, as they tend to respond less well to treatment at this stage. Sometimes people taking treatment are unable to adhere to, or tolerate the side effects of drugs.

The epidemic has had a devastating impact on societies, economies and infrastructures. In countries most severely affected, life expectancy has been reduced by as much as 20 years. Young adults in their productive years are the most at-risk population, so many countries have faced a slow-down in economic growth and an increase in household poverty. HIV and AIDS in Asia cause a greater loss of productivity than any other disease. An adult's most productive years are also their most reproductive and so many of the age group who have died from AIDS have left children behind. In sub-Saharan Africa the AIDS epidemic has orphaned nearly 15 million children.

In recent years, the response to the epidemic has been intensified; from 2002-2008 spending on HIV and AIDS in low- and middle-income countries increased 6-fold. Since 2008, spending has not increased so substantially, but it is still significantly higher than it was before 2002. The number of people on antiretroviral treatment has increased, the annual number of AIDS deaths has declined, and the global percentage of people infected with HIV has stabilized.

However, recent achievements should not lead to complacent attitudes. In all parts of the world, people living with HIV still face AIDS related stigma and discrimination, and many people still cannot access sufficient HIV treatment and care. In Eastern Europe infection rates are rising, and in Western Europe and America there are still tens of thousands of new infections each year – indicating that HIV prevention is just as important now as it ever has been. Prevention efforts that have proved to be effective need to be scaled-up and treatment targets reached. Commitments from national governments right down to the community level need to be intensified and subsequently met, so that one day the world might see an end to the global AIDS epidemic.

# Facebook

Facebook is a social networking service and the website was launched in February 2004. It is operated and privately owned by Facebook, Inc. As of July 2011, Facebook has more than 800 million active users. Users must register before using the site, after which they may create a personal profile, add other users as friends, and exchange messages, including automatic notifications when they update their profile. Additionally, users may join common-interest user groups, organized by workplace, school or college, or other characteristics, and categorize their friends into lists such as "People From Work" or "Close Friends". The name of the service stems from the colloquial name for the book given to students at the start of the academic year by some university administrations in the United States to help students get to know each other. Facebook allows any users who declare themselves to be at least 13 years old to become registered users of the site.

Facebook was founded by Mark Zuckerberg with his college roommates and fellow students Eduardo Saverin, Dustin Moskovitz and Chris Hughes. The website's membership was initially limited by the founders to Harvard students, but was expanded to other colleges in the Boston area, the Ivy League, and Stanford University. It gradually added support for students at various other universities before opening to high school students, and eventually to anyone aged thirteen and over. However, based on ConsumersReports.org on May 2011, there are 7.5 million children under thirteen with accounts, violating the site's terms of service.

Mark Zuckerberg wrote Facemash, the predecessor to Facebook, on October 28, 2003, while attending Harvard as a sophomore. According to The Harvard Crimson, the site was comparable to Hot or Not, and "used photos compiled from the online facebooks of nine houses, placing two next to each other at a time and asking users to choose the 'hotter' person".

To accomplish this, Zuckerberg hacked into the protected areas of Harvard's computer network and copied the houses' private dormitory ID images. Harvard at that time did not have a student "facebook" (a directory with photos and basic information). Facemash attracted 450 visitors and 22,000 photo-views in its first four hours online.

The site was quickly forwarded to several campus group list-servers, but was shut down a few days later by the Harvard administration. Zuckerberg was charged by the administration with breach of security, violating copyrights, and violating individual privacy, and faced expulsion. Ultimately, however, the charges were dropped. Zuckerberg expanded on this initial project that semester by creating a social study tool ahead of an art history final, by uploading 500 Augustan images to a Web site, with one image per page along with a comment section. He opened the site up to his classmates, and people started sharing their notes.

Facebook was incorporated in the summer of 2004, and the entrepreneur Sean Parker, who had been informally advising Zuckerberg, became the company's president. In June 2004, Facebook moved its base of operations to Palo Alto, California.

Facebook launched a high-school version in September 2005, which Zuckerberg called the next logical step. At that time, high-school networks required an invitation to join. Facebook later expanded membership eligibility to employees of several companies, including Apple Inc. and Microsoft. Facebook was then opened on September 26, 2006, to everyone of age 13 and older with a valid email address.

# Twitter

Twitter is an online social networking service and micro-blogging service that enables its users to send and read text-based posts of up to 140 characters, known as "tweets". It was created in March 2006 by Jack Dorsey and launched that July. The service rapidly gained worldwide popularity, with over 300 million users as of 2011, generating over 300 million tweets and handling over 1.6 billion search queries per day. It has been described as "the SMS of the Internet".

Twitter Inc. is based in San Francisco, with additional servers and offices in New York City.Twitter's origins lie in a "daylong brainstorming session" held by board members of the podcasting company Odeo. Dorsey introduced the idea of an individual using an SMS service to communicate with a small group. The original project code name for the service was twttr, an idea that Williams later ascribed to Noah Glass, inspired by Flickr and the five-character length of American SMS short codes.

The tipping point for Twitter's popularity was the 2007 South by Southwest (SXSW) festival. During the event, Twitter usage increased from 20,000 tweets per day to 60,000.

In August 2010, the company appointed Adam Bain as President of Revenue from News Corp.'s Fox Audience Network.

On September 14, 2010, Twitter launched a redesigned site including a new logo.

The company experienced rapid growth. It had 400,000 tweets posted per quarter in 2007. This grew to 100 million tweets posted per quarter in 2008. In February 2010, Twitter users were sending 50 million tweets per day. By March 2010, the company recorded over 70,000 registered applications. As of June 2010, about 65 million tweets were posted each day, equaling about 750 tweets sent each second, according to Twitter. As noted on Compete.com, Twitter moved up to the thirdhighest-ranking social networking site in January 2009 from its previous rank of twenty-second.

Twitter's usage spikes during prominent events. For example, a record was set during the 2010 FIFA World Cup when fans wrote 2,940 tweets per second in the thirty-second period after Japan scored against Cameroon on June 14, 2010. The record was broken again when 3,085 tweets per second were posted after the Los Angeles Lakers' victory in the 2010 NBA Finals on June 17, 2010, and then again at the close of Japan's victory over Denmark in the World Cup when users published 3,283 tweets per second. The current record was set during the 2011 FIFA Women's World Cup Final between Japan and the United States, when 7,196 tweets per second were published. When American singer Michael Jackson died on June 25, 2009, Twitter servers crashed after users were updating their status to include the words "Michael Jackson" at a rate of 100,000 tweets per hour.

# Anna and Jan Lokpal Bill

The Jan Lokpal Bill, also referred to as the citizens' ombudsman bill, is a proposed independent anti-corruption law in India. Anti-corruption social activists proposed it as a more effective improvement to the original Lokpal bill, which is currently being proposed by the Government of India.

The Jan Lokpal Bill aims to effectively deter corruption, redress grievances of citizens, and protect whistle-blowers. If made into law, the bill would create an independent ombudsman body called the Lokpal (Sanskrit: protector of the people). It would be empowered to register and investigate complaints of corruption against politicians and bureaucrats without prior government approval.

In April 2011, civil activist Anna Hazare started a Satyagraha movement by commencing an indefinite fast in New Delhi to demand the passing of the bill. Following Hazare's four day hunger strike, Indian Prime Minister Manmohan Singh stated that the bill would be re-introduced in the 2011 monsoon session of the Parliament. The Indian government went on to propose its own version in the parliament, which the activists rejected on the grounds of not being sufficiently effective, and called it a "toothless bill".

The first version of the Lokpal Bill drafted by the Government of India in 2010 was considered ineffective by anti-corruption activists from the civil society. These activists, under the banner of India against Corruption, came together to draft a citizen's version of the Lokpal Bill later called the Jan Lokpal. Public awareness drives and protest marches were carried out to campaign for the bill. However, public support for the Jan Lokpal Bill draft started gathering steam after Anna Hazare, a noted Gandhian announced that he would hold an indefinite fast from 5 April, 2011 for the passing of the Lokpal/Jan Lokpal bill.

To dissuade Hazare from going on an indefinite hunger strike, the Prime Minister's Office directed the ministries of personnel and law to examine how the views of society activists can be included in the Lokpal Bill. On 5 April, the National Advisory Council rejected the Lokpal bill drafted by the government. Union Human Resource Development Minister Kapil Sibal then met social activists Swami Agnivesh and Arvind Kejriwal on 7 April to find ways to bridge differences over the bill. However, no consensus could be reached on 7 April owing to several differences of opinion between the social activists and the Government.

On 7 April, 2011 Anna Hazare called for a Jail Bharo Andolan (translation: Fill jail movement) from 13 April, 2011 to protest against Government's rejection of their demands. Anna Hazare also claimed that his group has received six crore (60 million) text messages of support and that he had further backing from a large number of Internet activists. The outpouring of support was largely free of political overtones; political parties were specifically discouraged from participating in the movement. The fast ended on 9 April, 2011, after 98 hours, when the Government accepted most demands due to public pressure. Anna Hazare set a 15 August deadline for the passing of the bill in the Parliament, failing which he would start a hunger strike from 16 August. The fast also led to the Government of India agreeing to setting up a Joint Drafting Committee, which would complete its work by 30 June.

However, the Joint Drafting Committee failed to reach a conclusion and the five members of the Government on the panel came up with their own version of the bill, which was considered by Anna and his team as weak and will facilitate the corrupt to go free apart from several other differences. To protest against this, Anna Hazare announced an "Indefinite Fast" (not to be confused with "Fast until death"). Anna and his team asked for permission from Delhi Police for their fast and agitation at Jantar Mantar or JP Park. Delhi Police gave its permission with certain conditions. These conditions were considered by team Anna as restrictive and against the fundamental constitutional rights and they decided to defy the conditions. Delhi Police imposed sec 144 CrPC.

On 16 Aug, Anna Hazare was taken into preventive custody by Delhi Police. Senior officers of Delhi Police reached Anna Hazare's flat early in the morning and informed him that he could not leave his home. However, Hazare turned down the request following which he was detained. Anna in his recorded address to the nation before his arrest asked his supporters not to stop the agitation and urged the protesters to remain peaceful. Other members of "India Against Corruption", Arvind Kejriwal, Kiran Bedi, Kumar Vishwas and Manish Sisodia were also taken into preventive custody. Kiran Bedi described the situation as resembling a kind of Emergency (referring to the Emergency imposed in 1975 by the Indira Gandhi Govt.).

The arrest resulted in huge public outcry and under pressure the government released him in the evening of 16 Aug 2011. However, Anna Hazare refused to come out of Jail, starting his indefinite fast from Jail itself. Manish Sisodia explained his situation as, "Anna said that he left home to go to JP Park to conduct his fast and that is exactly where he would go from here (Tihar Jail). He has refused to be released till he is given a written, unconditional permission". Unwilling to use forces owing to the sensitive nature of the case, the jail authorities had no option but to let Anna spend the night inside Tihar. Later on 17 Aug, Delhi Police permitted Anna Hazare and team to use the Ramlila Maidan for the proposed fast and agitation withdrawing most of the contentious provisions they had imposed earlier. The indefinite fast and agitation began in Ramlila Maidan, New Delhi, and went on for around 288 hours (12 days from 16 August, 2011 to 28 August, 2011). Some of the Lokpal drafting committee members became dissatisfied with Hazare's tactics as the hunger strike went on for the 11th day.

Parliamentary actions on the proposed legislation

On 27 August 2011, a special and all exclusive session of Parliament was conducted and a resolution was unanimously passed after deliberations in both the houses of Indian Parliament by sense of the house. Anna Hazare, civil rights activists along with protestors at site of the fast welcomed this development on being informed, terming it as a battle "half won" while ending the protest.

●●

# FDI in Retail in India 2011

According to the current regulatory regime, retail trading (except under single-brand product retailing – FDI up to 51 per cent, under the Government route) is prohibited in India, which means for a company to get overseas money pumped in, products sold by it to the general public should only be of a 'single-brand'; this condition being in addition to a few other conditions to be adhered to.

India being a signatory to World Trade Organization's General Agreement on Trade in Services, which include wholesale and retailing services, had to open up the retail trade sector to foreign investment. There were initial reservations towards opening up of retail sector arising from fear of job losses, procurement from international market, competition and loss of entrepreneurial opportunities. However, the government in a series of moves has opened up the retail sector slowly to Foreign Direct Investment ("FDI").

Foreign investors are open to invest in India, except few sectors/activities, for which approval from the RBI or Foreign Investment Promotion Board ('FIPB') would be needed.The government has also not defined the term 'multi brand'. FDI in Multi Brand retail means that a retail store with foreign investment can sell multiple brands.

The recent clamor about opening up the retail sector to Foreign Direct Investment (FDI) becomes a very sensitive issue, the most important factor against FDI driven "modern retailing" is that it is labour displacing to the extent that it can only expand by destroying the traditional retail sector. This is because the primary task of government in India is still to provide livelihoods and not create so called efficiencies of scale by creating redundancies. As per present regulations, no FDI is permitted in retail trade in India. Allowing 49% or 26% FDI (which have been the proposed figures till date) will have immediate and direct consequences. Entry of foreign players now will most definitely disrupt the current balance of the economy; will render millions of small retailers jobless by closing the small slit of opportunity available to them. Retailing is not an activity that can boost GDP by itself. It is only an intermediate value-adding process. If there aren't any goods being manufactured, then there will not be many goods to be retailed! This underlines the importance of manufacturing in a developing economy.

Global retailers have already been sourcing from India; the opening up of the retail sector to the FDI has been fraught with political challenges. With politicians arguing that the global retailers will put thousands of small local players and fledging domestic chains out of business. The only opening in the retail sector so far has been to allow 51% foreign stakes in single branc consumer stores, private labels, high tech items/ items requiring specialized after sales service, medical and diagnostic items and items sourced from Indian small sector (manufactured with technology provided by the foreign collaborations). Parties supporting the FDI suggest that the FDI in retail should be opened in a gradual/ phased manner, such that it can promote competition and contribute to the growth of the Indian economy. The impact of the FDI would benefit the end user of the consumer to a great extent and will help to generate a decent amount of employment as more and more entrepreneurs would be coming forward to invest and taste the new generation in retail marketing. The opening of FDI should be designed in such a way that many sectors – including agriculture, food processing, manufacturing, packaging and logistics would reap benefits.

●●

# Workplace Problems that Women employees face

Women have no longer restricted themselves to cliché jobs which were typically meant for them, be it nursing, teaching, clerical, secretarial, etc. Today's women have reached senior positions in sectors which were traditionally meant to be male-dominated. While we have women at the armed forces, we also see women who have also marked themselves as successful sales professionals. New age work environments have led to newer sets of challenges for the Indian working women. Human Capital explores some of the new age problems and how today's women professionals and their employers have gone through a paradigm shift in handling gender based challenges.

Ever sector has its unique set of problems For instance, a woman professional in sales would face completely different set of problems than her counterpart in a technology sector. Neelam Doctor, a sales manager in a leading IT company shares that her challenges are more personal than organizational. Her job profile demands working at odd hours and meeting clients over a drink. In such a scenario, she is forced to take a male colleague along, though she is the one who is striking the deal. Often she has to share her successes with the male colleague.

If in sales, women professionals have to share their successes with male counterparts, in the technology sector, women have to make extra efforts to prove their smartness. As Richa Dhandhania says, men are generally perceived to be tech savvy, which might also hold true. However, women are equally skilled. Even then women have to try harder to break this myth and increase their efficiency. Besides, women have lot of other skills, which often goes unnoticed. She is wishful that sooner or later, her senior will realize that these skill sets are essential for smoother functioning.

In this new age work environment, where there is gender equality and women are given equal opportunities to learn and grow, women professionals in several sectors continue to face glass ceiling.There is a common perception that women come with additional baggage. If they are married, they can't stay for long durations at work, because they have a house to look after. If they are single, sooner or later they will be married, and won't be able to take the work load, hence are not considered for promotions, paid differently for the same work in comparison to her male counterparts, often excluded from informal networks, or discriminated against, based on the number of hours they work, etc.

Many a times the only limit is one's own strength. Like women, men too have their own set of challenges. Not every woman faces challenges, however, there are common challenges that certain women face at workplaces all over the world – the NEED to prove their credibility amongst their peers (mostly men) resulting in difficulty in getting visibility and being overly ambitious gets the lady branded as a feminist.

If there is a problem, the answer cannot be far away. It is essential to realize that every issue has two facets in every organization. One side is women being treated as lesser knowledgeable in terms of domain expertise due to pre-conceived notions. On the other hand owing to women's sensitive nature and the ability to multi-task, they are considered as better managers than male employees. This fact is further strengthened by Richa who is of the opinion that what matters is that one should be equally good in all skills no matter which gender you belong, to climb the ladder.

However, what came as a surprise was that women employees no longer blamed the organization or considered themselves to be any lesser than men. They accepted their limitations and worked towards a better tomorrow. When a number of women professionals were asked to comment if their gender hampered their growth in the organization? The responses were eye openers. Some women said they did not think their organization looks at them from the gender perspective. Similarly, another employee opines that never ever was any opportunity denied to anyone in the organization because of being a woman. Challenges if any, have been common to both male and female employees, and these challenges have provided multiple growth opportunities.

Organizations such as HP, DELL, GE, IBM, Mindtree have women-friendly policies in place and are continually striving to create family-friendly culture.

Organizations are sensitive towards the overall needs of their female staff and have devised multiple policies to help them strike the right work-life balance – health and wellness programs – preventative health check-up, health talks with special focus on women's health, tie-up with pre-school chain to provide subsidized childcare, extended maternity leave, work from home option, active women's forum that provides a platform for women employees to voice their opinion to name a few. Setting expectations early on by women employees projects the right message about their priorities and other people do not take them for granted.

Companies like HCL have their social connect site MEME which helps women on maternity or extended sabbaticals to stay connected with their project members, thereby facilitating their return to work smoothly. Organizations are also offering flexible-work arrangements for their women employees wherein they can choose a different work schedule that will help them meet their personal or family needs.

# Wrongful Termination Lawyers: Angels in Shinning Armours

The term 'wrongful termination' refers to the illegal sacking of an employee in a way that goes against the declarations made in a contract. Now this is often a very difficult situation considering that an individual's only source of income is threatened or taken away. When such a situation arises and the Employment Law has been broken, an employee has the right to appoint a wrongful termination lawyer to represent him against the company and get the justice he deserves. And if one gets good representation in the Court of Law, there is no reason why the matter will not be resolved or the complainant compensated.

Wrongful termination lawyers usually deal with various kinds of claims. If you are facing a similar situation, your case might fall into one or more of these categories.

## • Discrimination

If an employee has been fired because of his age, sex, race or any other personal reason that has nothing to do with the work, then he has the right to hire a discrimination lawyer to fight his case. Most companies have policies against discrimination and if they still indulge in it then there is bound to be serious consequences. However, it is important to note that there are different kinds of discriminations and not all of them could be specified in the contract. This is why sometimes grey areas can arise and this is when the wrongful termination attorney will have to look into this in great detail to find a solution.

## • Defamation

In some cases employers deliberately defame their employees because they want to terminate them for some reasons or the other. Often this is used as a cover over larger unresolved issue that needs to be examined closely. If defamation is combined with other clauses that are broken in the contract that the employee signed when he/she was initially hired, then the wrongful termination lawyers can put together a strong case.

## • Breach of Contract

Sometimes employees are hired for a particular function and for a particular time period. If the employer decides to terminate them without honouring what is stated in the contract then the employees can sue the employer for breaching the contract. In some cases all points are not explicitly stated in the contract while in others they are, that is why it is important to be careful when signing contracts with employers. Therefore, before signing a contract, it is advisable to have a good lawyer look at it to ensure that all possible problem areas have been covered to protect your interests.

## • Constructive Discharge

This situation arises when an employee quits his job because his employer instituted changes in the organization which made working there intolerable. However, in such cases, it is important for your wrongful termination lawyers to evaluate whether other employees would also have taken the decision to quit in such circumstances. The greater the objectivity that is used to view the case and the situation, the better it will be to determine the chances of getting a verdict in the employee's favour.

With an employee's livelihood under threat, it is definitely a challenging situation. But with good wrongful termination lawyers to look into the matter and advice on what should be the best course of action, one can be sure to have the matter resolved in no time at all.

●●

# Bankruptcy – A Lifeline for Debtors

Any discussion on bankruptcy is incomplete without understanding its meaning. When an individual or a business organization has no income and is unable to pay back its creditors, he can declare bankruptcy. In most situations, the debtor files for bankruptcy. There could be several reasons why one may file bankruptcy. The most obvious reason is financial trouble. Lay off is another reason one may file bankruptcy. However, one must remember that there is nothing criminal attached with bankruptcy. The sole purpose of declaring bankruptcy is to allow the debtor to begin afresh by taking care of most of his dues.

## Types of Bankruptcy

There are typically five types of bankruptcy, Chapter 7, 12, 13, 9 and 11. However; the most frequently filed ones are Chapter 7 and 13. For organizational and individual debtors, Chapter 7 takes care of all debts that are unsecured. It allows all or partial debts to be cleared using liquid assets. Any remaining debts are then discharged.

Chapter 13 allows the debtor to pay off the debt through a repayment plan and after it is done, any remaining debt is discharged.

Therefore, prior to filing for bankruptcy, one need to choose between the two, keeping in mind what is the best for them.

## Can Bankruptcy Help?

The question that now arises is can Bankruptcy help? The answer to this question is yes, but, Bankruptcy should always be the last option. If you are facing major financial crisis and into heavy financial liabilities, then filing for bankruptcy is a good option. Under these circumstances, the Court takes the responsibility of repaying all your dues. All types of bankruptcy last for twelve months. After this period is over, if any debts still remain unpaid, they are waived off.

## Conclusion

Bankruptcy will bail you from a critical financial situation but it will impact your credit score. In case you need any bankruptcy help, there are several bankruptcy attorneys, consumer forum, etc., who provide consultation free of cost. There are several law firms who provide free advices as well.

●●

# SEO....The New Tool to Enhance Your Website

SEO or Search Engine Optimization helps to optimize the use of your website with the help of search engines, which increases traffic and also optimizes the website. A good example of a search engine is Google. SEO is not just about search engines but also about choosing the right keywords. The next question in your mind must be...what is a key word? Well, the answer is very simple. When you are looking for specific information on the Internet, i.e., education, budget, etc., the first step is to type the relevant word into the search engine. A keyword comprises of a single word and a key phrase is of two or more words with commas in between. The keywords you choose must be relevant to your site and what it is selling.

## SEO Writing Made Easier

If you are interested in writing articles for SEO, the first thing is to choose the topic or keyword you want to write on. For instance, as a freelance writer, you want to write on SEO articles, think about all the probable words or phrases that relates to SEO writing. This is crucial in SEO article writing because these familiar words will drive the surfer towards your website.

After you have written the article, ensure that the keywords are there. The last step to SEO article writing is to ensure that the article is informative and is making sense.

## Writing Effective SEO Articles

Therefore, the best way to optimize traffic to your website is to write and submit SEO articles, which in turn improve the website's ranking. However, in SEO writing, it is not just about writing, rather it is about effective and grammatically correct articles which will not only drive traffic but also make them notice the content in your site.

So if you want your website to always be on the top whenever users are looking for any information relevant to your website, writing SEO articles which are good, informative, grammatically correct and relevant, then having them published on the Internet is the best and quickest way.

# Depression: a common Ailment among Youth

Our forefathers would be aggrieved to see the world as it stands today. The ever developing lifestyles are not without its share of diseases and illnesses, which were earlier unheard of. This modernity is accompanied by diversification and fragmentation. As we diversify, we isolate ourselves and thus, what remains are mere fragments, estranged from each other. This is the prime reason for all the psychological disorders that are arising today. The most common disorder that accompanies such an environment is called "clinical depression" or what is commonly called "depression". This however, differs from its general meaning as it does not fade away like normal depression; rather it has to be tackled with medical assistance. This disorder is common among youngsters. In fact, more and more young people are diagnosed with this disorder.

## What is Depression?

Depression is a kind of mental health disorder which an individual may suffer from. It is caused by many factors including the imbalance of chemicals in the brain. This disorder is characterised by constant and prolonged low mood which in turn affects a person's behaviour, character and self-esteem. A person suffering from depression is likely to lose interest in all his daily activities and may develop other disorders which could be detrimental to his health. A patient may be asked to undergo various laboratory tests however; there are no particular tests that can diagnose depression.

## Symptoms and Effects

A person suffering from depression experiences a feeling of low mood and low self-esteem. He usually experiences and displays feelings of unworthiness, hopelessness, despair and self-hatred. This in turn affects the character and behaviour of the person and his attitude towards life. He may distance himself from all social situations; lose interest in daily activities, have low memory and concentration. He prefers to be left alone at all times. Such an individual may even turn against himself, abuse his body by mutilating himself to a point of committing suicide or turn to drugs and alcohol abuse

Depression is often accompanied by lethargy, body aches, short temper and anxiety attacks. The sleep pattern also gets affected and the individual is likely to suffer from insomnia, hyper insomnia (excessive oversleeping) or wakes up too early. His appetite is also affected drastically, resulting in excessive weight loss due to decreased appetite or excessive weight gain due to overeating, which only aggravates depression.

In children, symptoms include irritability, low performance in school and disinterest in attending school. Their mood ranges from demanding, clingy, rebellious to insecure.

It is also alarming to know that individuals suffering from depression have shorter life expectancy than normal individuals.

## How Does Depression Develop In Young People?

Young people diagnosed with depression are of varying age groups. Some develop it as early as before their adolescence; some during their teens, while some after their adolescent years. There are many reasons that lead to depression in young people. Among children, the main reason is said to be post traumatic stress syndrome which occurs mostly in children from broken families, lack of attention from parents, poverty and social isolation. For teenagers, the most important factor is their growth process, which leads to their creation of self-image. Child abuse (physical, emotional and sexual) is another important factor which, if a child experiences, starts manifesting itself during their adolescent years. Stress is another factor which contributes to depression. This may be due to societal pressure, stress related to studies, which are often enforced by the educational institutions and by their families. For young people in their twenties, besides the usual factors, factors like personal dilemma which may result from their relationship with the opposite sex and the problem of decision-making regarding their future also contributes to depression.

## Treatment and Prevention

Depression is treatable. Patients suffering from this disorder are usually given anti-depressants in addition to psychotherapy and counselling. The patients are often prescribed anti-depressants that help the chemicals in the brain to gain balance again. In case medication and psychotherapy are not able to cure the problem, the last resort for treating patients suffering from depression is electroconvulsive therapy (ECT). Under the influence of anesthesia, this process makes use of electricity to trigger a seizure for therapeutic effect. Hospitalization is required only if there is a risk that the patient might cause harm to one's self or to others. The goal for treating people with depression is to make them feel that they are normal and they are loved and cared for.

Psychotherapists play an important role in the treatment of depression. "Talk therapy" is often used by therapists. This is a method wherein the therapist builds a relationship with the patient based on trust and allows the patient to address the reason of depression. This helps him to overcome the problem with a positive outlook. Other additional treatments may include exercise programs which also help in increasing the release of endorphins (chemicals responsible for the well-being of an individual) in the body. Motivational speeches are also effective in the treatment of depression. Music and art therapies are other effective ways of treating depression. Besides the prescribed treatments, it is important that the patient is constantly surrounded by his loved ones and it is also essential that his near and dear ones show that they love and care for him.

There are however, no prescribed ways to prevent depression because some reasons of depression are self-inflicted and others are not. Perhaps the most effective way to prevent and overcome depression is to have a positive attitude towards life.

# Indian Hockey – Near Extinction

Hockey was introduced in India by the British. The first hockey club came up in Calcutta in 1885-86 and soon Bombay and Punjab followed suit. It was earlier played only by the army personnel. India participated in the Olympics in 1928 and won the Gold in Hockey. India won 6 straight consecutive gold medals in Hockey till 1956. This period 1928-1956 is hence called the golden era of Indian Hockey. No Indian team till date has reached close to breaking this record. This period saw great players such as, Dhyan Chand, Balbir Singh, etc. India had in total won eight golds, one silver and two bronze medals in Olympics.

Getting adequate funds to help the Indian Hockey team to compete in the Olympics, have been a problem since 1936. However, leaders such as Jagdish Prasad and Naval Tata ensured that the Indian team made it to the Olympics. They managed funds from different sources and convinced the higher authorities to send the team to the Olympics. After Naval Tata, his successor Ashwini went a step further by selling his ancestral property to collect funds for the team. After he quit, the IHF has struggled to get a good leader who can stretch his limits for the team.

When India participated in the Olympics in 1932, there were as little as three teams participating in the competition. Since then the number has increased as well as the competition. The Indian Hockey's golden era came to an end when

Pakistan defeated India in the finals. It was not the players who failed rather it were the leadership and support which failed. The 1970s saw the advent of synthetic turf in international sports. This impacted their performance adversely because in India, synthetic turfs came six years later. Being the national game, there were very limited facilities for playing hockey in the country. The Government failed to promote the game in every school and college. People switched to playing Cricket which could be easily played on streets and small grounds which was not the case with Hockey. It became a sport which was played by few and hence affected the talent pool.

Youngsters lost interest in the sport and hence Hockey lost much of its fan base. The growing popularity of Cricket turned all investors towards it. India did manage to get talented players in the pool however, the IHF again failed to provide them salaries and incentives of a full-time job. There are many players who earn their living from this sport and treatment like this certainly affected their performances. When the much needed trainings were required, IHF kept changing the coaches. The result was that they couldn't even qualify for the 2008 Olympics for the first time after 1928.

Therefore, as Indians we need to focus our attention on laying a strong foundation of Hockey in our children. It is high time Hockey is treated and given the priority as our national sport. The facilities should be made available to engage as many youngsters as possible in the game. NGOs can play an important role in this. Existing players should be given due importance and incentives they deserve. Increasing awareness about the sport is also essential to increase its fan following. This will eventually bring corporate banners and would reduce the fund crunch.

●●